SECRETS OF DEATH VALLEY

MYSTERIES AND HAUNTS OF THE MOJAVE DESERT

Edited By Timothy Green Beckley

GLOBAL COMMUNICATIONS

Secrets of Death Valley
Mysteries and Haunts of the Mojave Desert

Compiled by Timothy Green Beckley
Additional Material by
George Van Tassel, Diane Tessman,
Regan Lee, Cactus Jim, Adam Gorightly

Copyright © 2010 – Global Communications, All Rights Reserved

ISBN-10: 1-60611-082-9
ISBN-13: 978-1-60611-082-9

Nonfiction
No part of this book may be reproduced, stored in retrieval system or transmitted in any form or by any means, electronic, mechanical, photocopying, recording, without express permission of the publisher. If you are the legitimate copyright holder of any material inadvertently used in this book please send a notice to this effect the "offending" material be will removed from future printings. The material utilized herein is reproduced for educational purposes and every effort has been made to verify that the material has been properly credited.

Timothy Green Beckley: Editorial Director
Carol Rodriguez: Publishers Assistant
Tim Swartz: Associate Editor
Sean Casteel: Editorial Assistant
Covert Art: Tim R. Swartz

For free catalog write:
Global Communications
P.O. Box 753
New Brunswick, NJ 08903

Free Subscription to Conspiracy Journal E-Mail Newsletter
www.conspiracyjournal.com

Contents

Midnight Madness In The Desert
    by Timothy Green Beckley .... - 5 -

Mojave
    by Starlight -- An Introduction To Mysteries of the Desert
    by Diane Tessman .... - 11 -

"From The Desert Sands, Cauldrons of Magic Will Spring"
    by Regan Lee .... - 15 -

A Brief History of Giant Rock
    by George W. Van Tassel .... - 21 -

I Rode a Flying Saucer
    by George W. Van Tassel .... - 27 -

The Haunted Desert
    by Cactus Jim .... - 77 -
        The Phantom Stage of Carrizo .... - 78 -
        The White Horse Ghost of Vallecito .... - 79 -
        The Ghost Lights of Borrego .... - 80 -
        The Eight-Foot Skeleton .... - 81 -
        Ghosts Dancers at Yaqui Well .... - 82 -

Charlie Manson's Death Valley Daze
    by Adam Gorightly .... - 85 -

1:17
    by Paul Dale Roberts, HPI Ghostwriter .... - 93 -

From the Sea To the Sand Lost Ships of the Desert
    by Harold O. Weight .... - 99 -

A Ghost of the Vikings?
    by Paul Wilhelm .... - 105 -

Mystery of the Desert
    by J. A. Guthrie .... - 109 -

The Lost Spanish Galleon
    by L. Burr Belden .... - 111 -

The Quest For The Lost Ship
    by the San Bernadino Guardian, September 10, 1870 .... - 113 -

The Serpent-Necked "Canoa"
    by Ed Stevens .... - 115 -

Butcherknife Ike and the Lost Ship
    by Adelaide Arnold .... - 119 -

The Story of the Pearl Ship
    by O. J. Fisk .... - 123 -

The Desert Ship
    by the San Bernadino Guardian, October 15, 1870 .... - 125 -

The Giants of Death Valley .... - 127 -
    Ancient Civilization Beneath Death Valley?
        by The San Diego Union .... - 127 -
    Expedition Reports Nine-Foot Skeletons
        by the "Hot Citizen" Nevada Paper .... - 130 -
    Article Concerning Same Cave Discovery
        by Different Men 10 to 15 Years Earlier .... - 132 -
    San Bernardino Caves - Kokoweef Caverns
        Sworn Statement Of E. P. Dorr .... - 135 -

Strange Alien Artifact Discovered In the Desert
    by Timothy Green Beckley .... - 139 -

Ghost Camels of the Desert
    by Joe Parzanse .... - 147 -
    Jake's Camels .... - 153 -

The Racetrack
    by U.S. National Park Service .... - 155 -

"Jesus Christ It's A Bigfoot!"
    by Timothy Green Beckley .... - 163 -

Life After Death In Death Valley
    by Timothy Green Beckley .... - 167 -

The Hollywood Stars Are Big and Bright and So Are ALL the UFOs!
    by Timothy Green Beckley .... - 175 -

There Is Still Gold In Them There Dunes .... - 183 -

The "Lost" Kokoweef Cavern and Money Pit Now "Found" .... - 187 -

Happy Trails
    by Timothy Green Beckley .... - 193 -

Leaping Lizzards and A Teleporting Leprechaun
    by Paul Dale Roberts .... - 199 -

Midnight Madness In The Desert
by Timothy Green Beckley

I'll never forget the first time I visited the desert at night.

I had taken a flight to San Diego, and driven the scenic route to Palm Springs where I spent a few days relaxing and doing interviews before heading south out of town to see the sites. I was hoping to find some therapeutic healing for my back and maybe some UFO chatter, and to this end I arranged to meet Robert Short in Desert Hot Springs for a round of hot tubing. Bobbie and I conversed on the phone several times about his UFO contacts in the desert and how a voice inside his head had directed him to take a certain road which lead to a really out of the way New Age conclave where he entered into an altered state of consciousness and allowed beings from outer space to channel messages through him. The place was known as Giant Rock, site of the largest standing bolder in the United States, and home to desert rat George Van Tassel who had once been the personal pilot to Howard Hughes. Van Tassel along with his wife in the 1950's and 60's, was manager of this small landing field and accompanying coffee shop which catered mainly to those looking to escape the big city and "hide out" among the sand dunes.

Desert Madness
A city slicker in the desert, Beckley looks high and low for any signs of life - human, animal or OTHERWISE!

The stars were like a brilliant prism and appeared so close that they reminded me of dazzling strings of golf balls. Too my eyes the universe looked as if it had just exploded. It was like someone had taken body paint and smeared it around and around over the intense blackness of space. The result being that when I peered heavenward I felt like I was surrounded – almost smothered -- by a multitude of splashing colors that were both mesmerizing and awe-inspiring.

A mysterious voice guided Robert Short of the Blue Rose Ministry to the desert and to Giant Rock where space messengers began using his vocal chords to transmit messages. He was one of the first of the UFO contactee "desert dwellers" the author made during his first trip to Desert Hot Springs.

My home was on the east coast, where while growing up, I had listened intently to the various UFO contactees that had appeared on the all night Long John Nebel radio talk show. Broadcasting from midnight to dawn over WOR in New York, 1440 on your AM dial, Long John's ratings thrived on the amazing stories told by the likes of George Adamski, George Van Tassel, Truman Bethrum and Daniel W. Fry, all of them claiming to have made contact with outer space beings who appeared remarkably human. As it turned out, the majority of these confrontations with alien beings took place in the Mojave Desert over three thousand miles away from where I was still living with my parents in a small town in New Jersey.

When I was ten years old, I had a sighting of two UFOs hovering and circling about directly above our house. So, at an young age, I quickly discerned that the universe was too vast for us to be all alone in it. Most positively, I concluded that we "humans" had not been singled out by the creator as the only place for life as we know it to exist in the universe. There was no question in my mind that there had to be other beings, possibly more advanced creatures, capable of stopping off for a cosmic rendezvous on their way to and fro across the vastness of time and space.

The flying saucer contactees made some mighty bold claims that were enough to blow rationality right out the window:

* That the planets in our solar system were inhabited!
* That life had developed throughout the universe pretty much the way it had on earth!
* And that if we learned to live in peace and harmony that eventually we would be welcome into the league of interplanetary nations.

Furthermore, the contactees said they regularly communicated via telepathy with our Space Brothers (so called because of their universalistic utopian attitudes), and even went for junkets to other planets onboard the disc and cigar shaped craft piloted by these majestic, almost angelic-like beings. And for the most part all of this took place in the high desert in such remote places as Joshua Tree, Giant Rock, Morongo, Indian Wells, Palm Desert, Landers, and Death Valley, California. A vast expanse of over 3,000 square miles that encompasses what is best known as the Mojave Desert, this is an area featuring the lowest, driest, and hottest locations in North America. The hottest temperature reported being on July 13 (my birthday), 1913 in the town of Furnace Creek where the thermometer registered a whopping 137 degrees.

From a dougout beneath Giant Rock, Van Tassel would channel the space being known as Ashtar who offered words of wisdom and comfort for earthlings in an age of nuclear weapons and the Cold War.

Now I don't want you to think this is a book all about flying saucers, spacemen from Mars, and beautiful women from Venus, (or wherever) – it definitely isn't! But, flying saucer "invaders" (friend or foe) definitely do play a major role in the weirdness of the Mojave Desert. Certainly, we would be negligent if we didn't cover the often times bewildering cosmic spectacle that is UFOlogy, along with phantom stagecoaches, giants who once lived under Death Valley, ghosts that haunt the wastelands, the horrific wanderings of Charles Manson (and his robotic, mind controlled, camp followers), and a long list of other camp fire tales that will boil your blood almost as quickly as the desert sun is guaranteed to do. Not to be forgotten are the fantastic stories of the desert rats and the prospectors whose memories define what has become a valuable part Americana.

Most of all, we do want to pay homage to the king of all dusty Mojave Desert story tellers, a man by the name of George Van Tassel who hooked up with Solgonda from "parts unknown" when a vehicle from outer space landed in the dead of night in close proximity to Giant Rock Airport of which Van Tassel was the proprietor of for many years, along with his wife. Though deceased for several decades now, the legend of Mr. Van Tassel lives on gaining momentum as a new generation is exposed to his odd life story. Over time George's claims to have received regular mental messages from a group of ever so friendly space beings known as the Ashtar Command, remain just as controversial as they ever were. "Back in the days," Van Tassel often fell into an altered state of consciousness in a room dug out under Giant Rock. It was while in a trance state that he allegedly received messages from UFO entities who took over his vocal chords speaking out loud to his followers seated in the subterranean cavern. Such communications were published in his journal, "Proceedings of the College of Universal Wisdom" and became the basis for several books.

Uppermost, Van Tassel constructed a round dome topped building called the "Integratron" near Giant Rock, based on instructions from his outer space contacts. The Integratron was designed to assist in the development of antigravity and time travel, something we must obtain, should we wish to leave the confines of earth. Though never officially completed, the eye catching structure can be found in the nearby town of Landers where it still receives visitors from all over the world. The current owners go out of their way to make the mysterious looking Integratron accessible for conclaves, and seminars. As part of our desert saga we are pleased to make available George Van Tassel's long out of print *Council of the Seven Lights* which stands as one of the classics in flying saucer contact literature.

So let us all hop onto our dune buggy or motorcycle and be sure to double lock the doors of our RV as we head out into the night in search of adventure – not knowing whatever will come our way.

Tim Beckley, Publisher
MRUFO8@hotmail.com
Global Communications
P.O. Box 753
New Brunswick, NJ 08903
www.conspiracyjournal.com

Famed Joshua Trees of the Mojave Desert

Standing in the brilliant noon day sun, Diane Tessman
visits the once majestic Giant Rock now showing
its graffiti covered face as if scared by modern man.

Mojave By Starlight —
An Introduction To Mysteries of the Desert
by Diane Tessman

It was a clear, cold night in California's Mojave Desert, and I had never been closer to the stars. Nowhere else on Planet Earth do the stars shine and twinkle so brightly. The sky stretched overhead like a mystical black blanket with shining crystals everywhere.

Two friends and I had driven into the Joshua Tree National Monument to go UFO hunting. The Monument is a national treasure in the magnificent high desert. Incredible rock formations and bizarrely-shaped Joshua trees dot the desert landscape. It is all very alien and yet so richly of Earth.

The three of us sat huddled under a blanket for about an hour and then decided to go home because of the cold. As we headed for the car, a large, brilliant, white light raced across the sky. Just as we struggled to tell each other it must have been a meteorite, it raced back in the opposite direction, stopping overhead for a second. It hovered just long enough for us to see smaller red, yellow, and blue lights in a circular pattern while its brilliant light, which illuminated the whole object, remained incandescent white.

Suddenly, it zoomed away, over the horizon from whence it came. We felt we had just witnessed something utterly incredible and otherworldly. We were speechless for a few moments, and then we couldn't stop talking about what we had just seen. I will never forget that UFO sighting which the Mojave Desert offered us that cold, starry night.

It is fact: The Mojave Desert never fails to provide us with chilling phantoms, mysterious ghosts, and unexplained hauntings. It also offers us unidentified star ships over head and alien encounters under the watchful eyes of monster rock formations. It tells us stories of Coyote Man and the dreaded Chupacabra, and it even sings of "Hotel California," where you can check out anytime you want but you can never leave.

The desert can be peaceful -- or it can be utterly violent. Savage lightning bolts captured streaking toward the ground near Joshua Tree by Diane Tessman.

When I lived near the town of Joshua Tree, California, I felt I was undergoing an intense two-year education in all things mysterious and alien. I could feel the ghosts at Giant Rock, that gigantic, enigmatic boulder a few miles from Landers, a village which suffered a devastating earthquake in the early 1990s.

The ghostly phantoms at Giant Rock were mostly Native American in "feel" and once I heard their flutes playing in the desert wind. Also, there was the spirit of George van Tassel.

In the 1950s and 1960s, tens of thousands of people streamed into Landers, blocking the highways for miles around. On they went to the flying saucer Mecca of Giant Rock, gathering with George van Tassel. At several of those gatherings, it is said that van Tassel, at will, summoned his extraterrestrial friends, who appeared overhead. Many people felt the alien contact and followed van Tassel's enlightened, brilliant teachings.

In 1951, his friends from Venus astrally transported van Tassel aboard their giant star ship and introduced him to "The Council of Seven Lights." The Council told him to build a structure in that energized area of California's high desert; they promised that this building would extend human life and help humans become enlightened.

Built according to the precise directions and requirements of van Tassel's alien friends, The Integratron still offers mind-blowing acoustics and experiences of an almost psychedelic nature.

I recently reread George van Tassel's book, "The Council of Seven Lights" and was amazed at the cosmic knowledge in its pages. It is a book which reflects not only metaphysical wisdom but which also delves into quantum physics within a spiritual format. Van Tassel was a genuine contactee of great experience and wisdom.

In 1995 and 1996, my daughter and I traveled almost daily to Giant Rock from our home in the town of Joshua Tree. We wandered around it, we meditated beside it. In the harsh sunlight of the desert day, the white quartz which composes Giant Rock gleamed and glistened. We tried to figure out how that huge boulder came to stand alone in the desert. There were no other boulders like it anywhere around. On distant desert hillsides, there were a few boulders which were much smaller than Giant Rock. Did Giant Rock roll across the desert from one of those hillsides miles away during an earthquake? Or did it come from the sky?

Giant Rock sometimes made us sad; there was ugly graffiti scrawled all over it. Hundreds of dirt bikes and motorcycles had wrecked the environment around it. There was also the infamous crack at the bottom caused by bonfires. The crack seemed to lead to a cave beneath the boulder. Rumor had it that a Nazi fugitive had hidden in this cave.

And so it was not surprising when, several years later, enigmatic Giant Rock suddenly split in half. When it did so, I had already moved to Iowa, but I remembered how sad the giant boulder itself seemed to be. No one respected it or seemed to remember the universal light work which had gone on around its domain. Giant Rock was a phenomenon of Mother Nature and perhaps a gift from outer space, and all humans could do now was to scrawl ugly words on it, scraping away the environment with their noisy bikes. One theory says that the vibrations from motorcycles helped split the mighty rock.

The tragedy of Giant Rock leads me to an insight on the mystical energy of California's Mojave Desert: This unique quantum energy can be used for enlightenment and goodness, or it can be used negatively.

The Manson Family's Spahn Ranch was in the Mojave.

It has long been joked that bodies murdered in Los Angeles end up in a hole in the Mojave.

The ghost of a rock musician who is said to have overdosed in the 1970s haunts the only motel in the town of Joshua Tree.

Yes, I do remember a feeling of panic sometimes in that hot desert sun, a feeling that the spirits there were restless. Coming home one noon, I saw a small child sitting under the Joshua tree across the road. The child was crying softly. I rushed over, only to have the child dematerialize.

My daughter witnessed a tribe of "restless spirits" one dark desert night as they seemed to be picking leaves off of one of the trees in our yard. She said they seemed confused and unhappy.

I researched various paranormal happenings for a video I did about Giant Rock and the Mojave. I traveled into Joshua Tree Monument to find the precise rock formation into which a teenage couple is said to have disappeared. I had just enjoyed the film "Picnic at Hanging Rock," which is the account of young girls on a picnic in Australia who disappeared without a trace into a mysterious rock formation.

The particular formation in Joshua Tree National Monument is actually two formations, standing right next to each other. Between them is a narrow "doorway" through which one can squeeze. Apparently the teenage couple went through the doorway and were never seen again. Their friends hurried through the same doorway minutes later, searching for them. Was there a dimensional portal which opened precisely as they went through, and which then closed again?

Mother Earth has given the Mojave Desert very unique and dynamic energies which give rise to endless paranormal events as well as beckoning visitors from other worlds and dimensions. There have been more UFO sightings in the Mojave than any other area on Earth.

It is past time that a book be devoted to telling a few of The Mojave's mysterious secrets. Enjoy.

Receive a FREE CHANGE TIMES BULLETIN
direct from Diane! Learn where the next big Earthquake will be. Receive urgent updates on drastic changes in Earth's ELECTROMAGNETIC FIELD and how to survive this catastrophe. Receive the very latest news on radical steps the government is taking. Be among the first to know of coming social upheaval and natural disasters including huge tsunamis.

Send your request to:
Diane Tessman, Box 352, St. Ansgar, IA 50472
Diane also offers personal, private counseling service!
and visit Diane's website: DianeTessman.com

"From The Desert Sands, Cauldrons of Magic Will Spring"
by Regan Lee

Many of the contactee experiences with extraterrestrials took place in the American deserts. The deserts as a place of mystical meetings with spirits from other realms is a setting known the world over. The desert has been the stage for other worldly encounters with Jinns, Space Visitors, Mary, religious deities and entities, and Dana Howard's meetings with the alien entity Diane was no exception to this idea of desert as spiritual landscape. As Diane said to Howard of this potent and ethereal location: "From the desert sands, cauldrons of magic will spring." It is in these silent and open settings of the California deserts in the Yucca Valley that Contactee Dana Howard met with the beautiful and wise Space Sister Diane, who called to Dana as other Space Visitors called to other contactees at the time. The is the same location where Giant Rock lives; home for George Van Tassel and for a time, a place for all those to gather who had encountered peaceful extraterrestrials who wanted to share their knowledge with humanity.

During these meetings in the sacred desert setting, Diane shared with Howard eclectic discourses on the coming changes for earth and humanity. These conversations followed much of the typical Space Brother and Sister message, which included warnings, -- no matter how lovingly or gently said -- for humanity to get it together to better meet the intense challenges soon to come: dramatic climate changes, structural changes to earth's geography, changes to the world economy and society's infrastructures. And last but not least, massive changes on a spiritual level. Diane's words, like many of the "aliens" during the contactee era, were words of love as well as warnings. Reading Over the Threshold today, which was written in 1957, is eerily prophetic, considering the climate changes, pole shifts, and economic fiascos we're currently experiencing.

The pull of the desert was a strong one for Dana, and called to her in profound ways. The setting of the desert underscores the mythic qualities of Dana Howard's experiences. There is something quietly mysterious about the desert; a perfect place to meet visitors from other realms. The desert is an isolated area of course, where such esoteric meetings can take place without detection or interruption. Dana Howard saw the desert as sacred; calling the desert a "holy altar." A perfect place, this holy setting, for Howard to meet with her muse, her mentor, her personal astral guide. Dana wrote that the desert was her "favorite retreat," a place where she could "seek seclusion." It is in the desert that our world intersects with other realms normally undetected. Diane explains the power of the desert to Dana: "Our deserts are the recognized last frontiers of hope. Out where the veil is thin . . .(humanity can) readily be nursed back to health again." Somehow, some manifestation of an "other" came through that veil to communicate with Dana. It's possible the wide open areas of the desert, remote and fairly unbothered, act as portals between worlds. Someone once told me to "think about the sand" in relation to the desert setting and contactee encounters. What is the sand made of? Silica, crystals, quartz. Crystals are transmitters; they hold and impart information. It's not a coincidence humans have been using quartz crystals in not only technological ways but esoteric ways as well. As Venusian Diane tells Dana:

"The deserts are the storehouses of the earth's precious minerals. Those who love the desert love it with a passion they cannot explain. At night there is an endless tune from the melodies of nature -- voices and sounds from the desert's own soul...brilliant by day with its billions of granules of golden sand, by night the spacious filament alive with twinkling stars."

The desert setting as a heavenly meeting space for alien visitors (whether that alien literally comes from Venus, or comes forth from another realm) was a powerful one for Howard. The desert, for Howard, was "in one's blood," and while she found the desert safe, peaceful and inspiring, she was also aware of the "desert violence" at times. Yet the desert always remained sacred: "But, with it all, when the desert was in one's blood, it was there forever." The spiritual aspect of these meetings, while similar to many of the Contactee encounters, seems to have been dramatically potent for Dana Howard. The very desert itself was "alive with spiritualized energy," seemingly acting as a magnet, pulling Diane from the ether onto the desert floor. Dana describes how Diane sometimes seemed to slowly dematerialize; sinking "into the earth," or where her "presence was fading rapidly . . . to sink back into the sandy earth" once more.

It might be tempting to have an easy and glib response to stories like Dana Howard's; that she spent too much time in the desert sun. After all, what ridiculous stories!!! Meetings with a female Venusian named Diane; stories of subterranean demons, turning thought forms into physical reality ,the secrets of remaining young, flying saucers, -- clearly the ranting of a kook, some could say. There were certainly shady aspects to many of the contactee episodes, and yet, even with the often goofy circus type aura surrounding the contactee phenomena, synchronicities, UFO sightings, and other anomalous events occurred enough to make it difficult to dismiss these encounters outright. Add to this mix of mystically life changing shifts with the bizarre claims and ridiculous antics of both contactees and the aliens is the fact that the government was interested in contactees.

Many of the contactees had some kind of military connection, and it's possible the desert setting was a convenient one for military psy-ops manipulations. We can't say for certain if Howard was some sort of shadow government mind control experiment or not. There were others who also saw the entity Diane; some independently of Dana. Witnesses saw flying saucers in the desert in context of Howard's experiences. Like other contactee stories, which are often ludicrous on the surface, there are also things that aren't so easy to dismiss outright. Too many "coincidences" occur, too many experiences, including independent witness accounts of UFO sightings, to entirely reject the contactee experiences, including Dana Howard's.

In some ways, Dana Howard's meetings with Diane can be compared to BVM appearances. Like the figure Mary in Marian apparitions, Diane refers to Dana as "my daughter" numerous times. Howard describes Diane's "exquisite perfumes" and Diane's words were both warnings and urgings for humanity to reach a higher level of vibration, to work on compassion and self knowledge.

Howard was aware of the traditional religious aspects of the desert as sacred place. The Yucca Valley is home to Desert Christ Park; where a collection of statues based on Biblical holy figures silently witness numerous visitors throughout the year. Dana meets Diane here as well; where the message of a universal creed is preached, and the power of the desert is once again stressed. "...it is ever in the sacred areas you will find the spiritual treasures. All of God's children seek the seclusion of the wilderness in days of stress. . . The shrines of the earth serve as a focal point in consciousness..."

It's possible Diane was of the same energy as the energy that gives us Marian apparitions and other "high strangeness" encounters, (and not literally a "Venusian" at all). Something very powerful happened to Dana Howard in the magical California deserts that stirred her creatively and spiritually. In fact, Diane, whoever or whatever she was, seemed deeply connected to Nature. Dana Howard's first meeting with Diane was in 1939 in the woods; as she wrote in her book Diane: She Came From Venus (1956):

> ...my vision was directed to a gnarled old tree overlooking the antediluvian hills. Leaning casually against the grotesque trunk was a woman being of unsurpassed loveliness. Her head was radiant with a crown of fire, strands of golden hair cascading gently over her beautiful, slightly olive-tinted shoulders. The strange mystic light flooding her dark, prophetic eyes, added a wishful something to all her other charms.

Nature spirit, Venusian, Mary, a Trickster -- Diane was a vivid energy that others besides Dana Howard also experienced in the desert "altars in the wilderness" where "cauldrons of magic" did spring forth, and, whatever the force was that was Diane, compelled Dana Howard to share with us.

Regan Lee
Oregon, 2010

Regan Lee is a UFO witnesses and writes on her own UFO related sightings and experiences, as well as the UFO phenomena in general.

Regan's interests are not limited to the UFO phenomena, but include paranormal, crypto zoological and esoteric subjects. One of her specialties is the contactee movement and the golden age of flying saucers.
www.orangeorb.net

**Titles available from Global Communications
by Dana Howard include:
Up Rainbow Hill and
Over The Threshold
with others to come.**

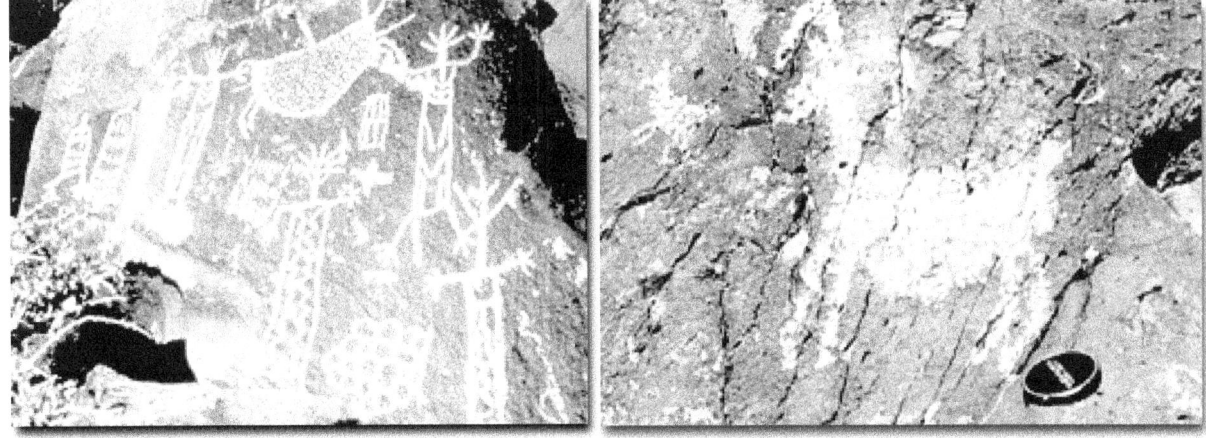

Native American petroglyphs depict many different Mojave species. The desert bighorn sheep has a particularly prominent place in the right photo above. Photo Credit: RICHARD BROOK, BLM

A Brief History of Giant Rock
by George W. Van Tassel

When I came out here in 1947, I became a close friend of Charlie Reche. Later, I bought Charlie's property, which was known as Reche's Wells.

Charlie Reche had been here since 1887, at which time the people living in the area were all Indians. Most of the information I gathered concerning the history of Giant Rock was from both the Indians and Charlie Reche. So I figure this information is right from the horse's mouth, so to speak, because they were the ones who were here before it became what it is now.

An early model with Van Tassel showing how the "time machine in the desert" would be constructed with no metal, not even nails.

According to the Indians, this was an Indian Holy Ground, where the north and south tribes met annually. The Chiefs held their séances and meetings close by the Big Rock, which they called the "Great Stone," because to them it symbolized the Great Spirit, as it was the largest single object in the area. Today, it is still known as the largest single boulder in the world.

The Indians assembled for their meetings here for up to three days at a time. During their meetings, none of the tribesmen were allowed close by as the meetings, per se, were actually a collection of the Chiefs and the VIPs in the tribe. The rest of the people in the tribe had to camp about a mile or so away so as not to be near the actual meeting place.

I had the honor of being able to speak to the son of an Indian Chief. This man was ten years old when his father put a mark on the Giant Rock, on the north side. The Indians called this mark "the Sign of the Scorpion." To the Indian's understanding, this means a good place. Also, wherever an Indian Chief put a sign, no other Indian was allowed to put other signs. This being the reason for only the one sign on the big Rock.

Whenever one finds an area where there are numerous Indian hieroglyphics on the rocks, this is an area where Indian children have been practicing the art.

Charlie Reche, having homesteaded here in 1887, was allowed the privilege of meeting with the Indians many times. Reche's homestead included the area where the Integratron now stands, as well as several acres besides.

In 1930, while I was still in Santa Monica, a very interesting person arrived at my uncle's garage. This fellow had taken up prospecting because he had been in a fishing fleet and also in the Merchant Marine, and as a result had acquired too much moisture in his lungs. Therefore, under doctor's orders, he had discontinued these activities where he had to be in fog and moisture all the time. He had a four cylinder Essex car which had a rod knocking in the engine and he had no money.

My uncle, Glenn Paine, had his garage on 2nd Street, just off of Broadway in Santa Monica, across from the Carmel Hotel. He engaged mostly in the selling of overnight parking for the hotel inside his garage. He also did repair work and was a Buick specialist.

When I came to California from Ohio, in 1930, to see my uncle, he needed someone to help him. So I stayed with him and that's how I happened to be there.

This man I spoke of happened to be Frank Critzer. When he came into my uncle's garage, he was looking for someone to correct that rod knock in his Essex, who would do it without charge.

Being interested in mining and having a period of lull during the depression, we just happened to have a little time on our hands when this fellow drove in with his Essex. So, that same day we took him to lunch with us. We discovered he was a very intelligent person and that he did know quite a lot about prospecting. Thus, in the course of getting acquainted we became instant buddies, so to speak. My uncle allowed him to sleep in the garage and we repaired his Essex.

When Frank Critzer was ready to leave, we gave him $30.00, which was a lot of money in those days. We also stocked his car full of canned goods and headed him out. He told us that wherever he would settle down then he'd write to us, and also that we would be included in any mining claims he should happen to declare.

A year went by before we finally heard from him. We had practically given up on him when we received a letter in which he had drawn a map showing how to get to Giant Rock. The following weekend my uncle and I went to Giant Rock to see him.

Frank had already started to dig under the big Rock to make a place to live. Banning was the closest town in which one could purchase supplies for building, so Frank was getting by with what was there. Too, he had only squatter's rights and a mining claim on Giant Rock. He didn't own the property, for it was government land. By digging under the Rock he could have a place to live without having to purchase materials to amount to anything.

Van Tassel standing before a sign proclaiming the opening of his organization the Ministry of Universal Wisdom.

Frank had shrewdness and comprehension, so he reasoned that if he dug a room under the north side of the Giant Rock, the boulder would take all summer getting warm and hold the warmth beneath it during the winter. By the same reasoning, the Rock would get cold during the winter and keep the room temperature cool during the summer. Thus there would be little need for heating or cooling. This would amount to six months' delayed thermal reaction.

This has proved to be good engineering on Frank's part because the maximum temperature under the Rock is 80°F without any refrigeration in the summer time, and a minimum of 55°F in the winter time with no heating. The outside temperature will vary from approximately 25°F to 115°F.

The Giant Rock covers 5800 sq. ft. of ground and is 7 stories high. The rooms dug out from beneath it amount to approximately 400 sq. ft., so one can readily see that this is a very small fraction of the total area of the bottom side.

Frank was falsely accused of stealing dynamite, failing to register for the draft, and several other things, in 1942, while the US was at war with Germany. Having a German name, it was assumed by many people that he had to be a German spy in order to live in such a desolate place as Giant Rock.

The only radio Frank Critzer had was one that Charlie Korell had given him. I spoke to Charlie later about this as he made frequent trips to Giant Rock. The radio was a little 3 dial, A & B dry battery Atwater Kent, with the tubes exposed and no case around it. It wasn't any good for transmitting messages to Germany, although it was a superhetrodyne receiver.

The stories had generated from some people's erroneous thinking. Frank did have a German name. He had served in the German Navy as a mess boy on a German submarine in World War I. But he had come to our country, worked in our Merchant Marine, and was a naturalized citizen. Besides, he had no further affiliation with Germany whatsoever. But because he did have a big radio

Famous as a desert airport more than just planes were said to touch down here at Giant Rock.

antenna on top of the mountain, some people assumed he was using his radio for spying purposes and, without first checking with the FBI, these people started the rumor that Frank surely must be a spy. Consequently, in August of 1942, three deputies came to Giant Rock, supposedly to take Frank in for questioning.

I spent many weekends visiting with Frank at Giant Rock. Frank had a big kitchen table, and a big wood-burning cook stove, on which he prepared, cooked, and served German pancakes for anyone who happened to stop in. He usually had a case of two of dynamite and a partially opened case under the big kitchen table. We would put our feet on them when we were with him. He also had some caps, as he was doing some prospecting and dynamiting, and he knew how to use these things.

When the three deputies came to take Frank in, the first thing he noticed was that they were from Riverside County. Giant Rock being in

San Bernardino County and Frank being a man of principle, he knew they had no authority in this county and he told them so.

According to Bill Royal, who had brought the deputies out here -- as they didn't even know where Giant Rock was, Frank, after a lot of arguing, said that if they were going to take him in anyway, that he needed to get his coat. When he went into his living quarters beneath Giant Rock to get his coat, he pulled the 2 x 4 bar, which he had across the door on the inside to hold it in place, and thus barricaded the door. The deputies immediately assumed Frank was defying them, so they lobbed a tear gas grenade in through the north side window. The unfortunate part of this whole incident was that the grenade landed underneath that table, thus setting off the caps and dynamite. The explosion killed Frank Critzer, blew the windows out, and injured the deputies.

It may surprise some readers to know that Van Tassel was not the only individual to witness strange phenomenon at Giant Rock. A police officer took this picture during the annual UFO contactee convention held there.

Newspapers ran the story that he was a German spy. I had personally talked with the FBI; they knew the newspaper stories were not true.

Frank had written a manuscript called the "Glass Age" which he'd given to a friend to type. In 1936 he had already in print all of the plastics we use today, and some of which we do not have yet. He was an advanced thinker in his own right, with a brilliant mind.

When I finally had the time from work to come to Giant Rock after reading about Frank's death in the newspapers, there was nothing left but the hole under the rock. All of Frank's belongings had been hauled away, including the 4 cylinder Essex. The place was literally stripped. I was working for Douglas Aircraft at the time, and about a month had passed before I could come to Giant Rock.

On numerous occasions, after the death of Frank, I came with my wife and family to spend our vacations here camping out -- because we all loved this place.

When the war ended in 1945, I made application to the Bureau of Land Management to acquire this property, and wanted to make and airport here. Frank had already cleared an area and many airplanes had landed. However, it wasn't on the airmaps. Being of hard decomposed granite, it is a perfect natural runway. But it was not until 1947 when the paperwork which was involved was finally completed [that] we were able to move to Giant Rock.

It was in 1953 when we began the weekly meditation meetings in the room under Giant Rock which led to the UFO contacts. This resulted in the information which led to the principles of rejuvenation and to the creation of the Integratron.

I operated the airport from 1947 until December 1975 at which time I sold it to Phyllis and John Brady, who in turn turned it over to Jose Rodriguez and his family in 1977.

Giant Rock has been known world-wide for a long time for its unusual UFO activities and for the many unmatched annual Space Conventions which have been held here.

**Text courtesy of Cabot's Old Indian Pueblo Museum,
67-616 E. Desert View, Desert Hot Springs, CA 92240**

The Integratron

Mysteries and Haunts of the Mojave Desert - Secrets of Death Valley

I Rode a Flying Saucer!

•

THE MYSTERY OF THE FLYING SAUCERS REVEALED

through

GEORGE W. VAN TASSEL

•

Radioned to you by Other-World Intelligences in Reaction to Man's Destructive Action.

Copyright 1952
by
George W. Van Tassel

*"Man I have created
In the Light of My Oneness,
To Build unto Me.
Those who Destroy
My Manifested Beings and Creations,
Are in Darkness."*

The Integratron

The Author And "Time Machine."

PUBLISHER'S NOTE

Zooming across the skies and vanishing into outer space, the Flying Saucers present one of the most intriguing puzzles ever to face mankind.

In view of the wide-spread interest in the Flying Saucers we believe Mr. Van Tassel's solution to the mystery is most timely and intriguing. Coming as it does from a man with the careful good judgment of a flight test engineer, it warrants the most serious consideration. We have found Mr. Van Tassel to be a man of exceptional ability and vision.

Although some scientists hold that Flying Saucers may be due to natural phenomena and others maintain them to be of Russian or American manufacture, the greater number of scientists and laymen believe them to originate in other worlds than ours; that they are visitors from outer space. And why not? Are our scientists not planning to go to the moon in the near future? At any rate here is an intelligent account of a most unusual experience.

Is the fate of humanity threatened? Do the "saucer beings" have the answer? Will the destructive genius of man find its master in beings from outer space? Read the messages received at Giant Rock and draw your own conclusions.

Certain words occurring in the messages from the "saucer beings" call for some explanation that the reader may know just what they are talking about.

Shan denotes the earth.

Blaau is the name given to the Fourth Sector of the sector system of Vela, into which our solar system is moving.

Schare (pronounced *Share-ee*) is the name of a Saucer Station in space.

Ventlas is what the "saucer beings" call their "saucers."

As in most light induction communications and automatic writing the messages impressed by the communicating intelligence are often colored by the speech and language characteristics of the recipient.

In the case of Mr. Van Tassel the messages are received while he is in attunement with the vibratory frequency of the communicating intelligence and usually in a state of involuntary physical sensing, therefore being unaware of his audience. In some cases a partial perception of those around him is common. The mechanism of these receptions will be discussed more fully in a forthcoming book by Mr. Van Tassel entitled "The Council of the Seven Lights."

Franklin Thomas.

INTRODUCTION

The author is not interested in placing the contents of this writing before you to create fear, or to entertain you. The sole purpose of this book, is to attempt to get the readers to think for themselves.

One must realize that the continual building of bigger and better *means* of destruction must ultimately end in *some way, sometime.*

The minds of those who are immersed in the flood of their own creations certainly cannot be expected to think along lines that would oppose their own efforts. Whether they evolve the theory or design the mechanism or build the bomb that destroys, is of no concern to the author.

One is not concerned with the individual part that was played by each mind or hand that produced a bomb, while their loved ones are lying around them blown to bits.

Certainly any effort to end continual destruction on earth, before man destroys the earth itself, must come from an "outside" source. This is the reason for the importance of "signs in the skies," and of "flying saucers."

The author has observed the skies, and aircraft through the past thirty years. Born in Jefferson, Ohio, in 1910, raised in a normal home, by middle class parents, he entered aviation after high school in 1927 and served as airline mechanic four years, then worked in aircraft for Douglas eight and one-half years, Howard Hughes two and one-half years, and Lockheed Aircraft four and one-half years. During this twenty-year period of flying and flight test work the author's observations of other craft in the air has been almost continuous and daily. Now at the age of 42 years, he is living with his wife and three daughters, at Giant Rock, 16 miles north of the Twenty-nine Palms highway, at the Joshua Tree intersection. At present he is operating a commercial airport, resort and guest ranch.

Giant Rock Airport has a background of phoney spy stories a mile long. The previous occupant of Giant Rock, a man named Frank Critzer, was unfortunate enough to have a German name while the United States was at war with Germany in World War II. Several individuals who didn't like the way he parted his hair, caused him to be investigated numerous times and he was killed in 1942 by a blast of dynamite, supposedly by his own hand. The author "grubstaked" this man Critzer in 1930 and spent many week ends with him at Giant Rock.

Observing the great physical strength, calm demeanor and peace of mind displayed by Critzer, the author acquired a desire to live at Giant Rock. Through eight months of flight test work with Howard Hughes at Harper Dry Lake near Barstow, California, the author was sold on the clean air, the intense quiet nights and outdoor living in the desert.

Having acquired the property at Giant Rock from the government, the author learned to *feel* the freedom of living with nature. Four and a half years of this natural freedom made it possible for the author to find his true being.

Today man builds the means to destroy. Will he be faced with the rebound tomorrow?

Realize that you and your loved ones are at present victims of continual destructive influences. Try to find the way out.

In reading this book, listen to that "inner voice" that will cause you to recognize truth when it appears.

Anyone who can break the bonds of automatic living, in the confusion of cities and "civilization," can find the *reality* of his eternal self.

George W. Van Tassel.

Desert Cave Entrance

I RODE A FLYING SAUCER!

I rode a flying saucer! What person would be stupid enough to make such a statement to the public? I believe I am the first person whose stupidity would expect anyone to believe such a statement.

My moronic attempt to convince anyone is only exceeded by the saucer beings themselves. You see, *I* don't claim to have been aboard a flying saucer; the intelligences that operate the saucers, *claim I was aboard.*

I am not claiming anything. I only place the information in this writing before you, because I believe "all things are possible," in my Creator's Universe. *I* can't even verify this belief to you, yet multitudes believe it.

There is no question left in anyone's mind as to whether the "saucers" are real. The Air Force has chased them. Radar instruments have picked them up on their scopes. Thousands of people have seen them.

If they exist (and a man-made instrument called radar has detected and followed them), what is so fantastic in believing that an *instrument made by the Creator* of this endless universe, has also detected them, and received intelligent communication from them?

Scientists from all branches of science have advanced theories by the dozens about the "saucers."

Spinning particles or "ions," magnetic lines of force, little men, speeds beyond anything our aircraft can do, are among the explanations offered, in some cases by famous scientists.

These trained minds devise and describe all manner of means by which the saucers travel. They accept the laws of action and re-action, but their efforts to explain the saucers' *motion* ends with *motion*. Science explains that nothing can move without the existence of force to move it. Science presents laws of gravitation, inertia, momentum, etc. To defy these forces requires *directed intelligent control of an opposing force*. Man on this planet flies through the *unseen* air, by overcoming gravity. No one can *see* what holds an airplane up. Yet millions trust this *unseen substance,* as a "track" to travel on. They also *breathe* this *unseen substance* to live. The content of air that maintains life did not get there by some haphazard chance. It was caused to be there.

The *motion* of a saucer must also be *caused by intelligence* to defy our accepted laws of gravitation. Science has only explained the saucers to the public *in effect*. Cause has been shoved into a background of sensationalism. Scientists say they are spinning "ions" of light particles. In order to "spin," or move at all, requires a *cause,* an *intelligence,* to start something spinning. Nothing moves of itself.

Man views television, listens to radio, rides in airplanes, and *causes* all these things to operate through, or on, or in an *unseen* medium. He cannot even see his own *thought,* the *unseen* intelligence that *caused* these material things to be manufactured. Yet man goes through his daily life *accepting this unseen intelligence* without question.

Now that even my own reasoning has accepted my own thoughts, which are not visible, maybe I can find out what *causes* this thing called thought.

After deliberately spending much time with my thoughts, I became acquainted with this *unseen* portion of myself. I discovered the life substance of my true identity, my seventh sense—the sense of *be-ing*.

Throughout the multitudes of people on this tiny speck of matter in space the belief is predominant that each will "go to heaven" when they die.

Why do they *feel* this is true? Because a preacher or priest, or rabbi says it is so? No! Because the *truth* of eternal *life* is inherent within them. *It is* themselves, in true reality, *unseen*. It is that portion of the created "image" of *unseen God, the substance of cosmic atomic composition of true light intelligence,* the part of you that recognizes right from wrong, that whispers to your brain.

Science cannot, now or ever, see life or intelligence, in its pure state. Yet each individual can find it, within himself. But each must *cause* the *effort* to *create* the *effect*.

Through the process of causing myself to study the thing that makes me tick, I found an *instrument that is perfect*. It is part of the *one perfect cause* that created it. With this unfailing, indestructible, eternal substance of *unseen intelligence,* I discovered I could *parallel* radio, airplanes, television and other material instruments and mechanisms. Not in the crude confines of smash-up, burn out or failure. *I am not limited* to our atmosphere to fly. I am receptive to *all vibrations* throughout space, without depending on a transmitting station to project man made pictures or sound. This is *true freedom.* I am not afraid to leave this dense material body. I have found *unlimited true life* while I am within the confines of its physical limits. The universe is mine to explore.

After *causing this effect to be within my control,* I soon discovered how to separate the true vibrations from the discords. Through one of these vibration receptions I was instructed, by *unseen intelligence,* to gather a few others who were interested. This I did, and we hold scheduled meetings, at regular times, *to consolidate our effort, in unity,* to add more *power,* to make the *receptivity* more sensitive and easier to control.

These meetings have been in progress for several years. Each vibration or transmission has to be tuned in, to receive it intelligibly. In the process of "dialing" these "wave-lengths," I seemed to have one that persisted in attuning itself to my "receiver."

I had become cautious, through experience, because I found many of the vibrations could "burn up my cabinet," my physical body.

This particular vibration is exceptionally powerful, and the co-operation I received from its source assisted me in many ways to gradually become accustomed to its power.

After I could receive this intelligence, in attunement, without physical discomfort, the beings of the vibration gave me the following information. It is given here exactly, in words of human understanding. As I receive the message, it is spoken from my physical "loud speaker," and recorded in shorthand.

Sincerely yours,

GEORGE W. VAN TASSEL

VIEW OF MONTE BLANCO.

Area of many desert gold and mineral mines

THE MESSAGES

Here are the messages received to the date of this writing. There are several others, but they would not be comprehended by the reading public.

January 6, 1952.

"I am Lutbunn, senior in command first wave, planet patrol, realms of Schare. We have your contact aboard 80,000 feet above this place. Your press will have more to report on your so-called flying saucers. We return your contact. Discontinue."

February 8, 1952.

"Greetings. I am senior in command, first wave planet patrol from the realms of Schare. We have been instructed to contact this point at any time you are in session. We bring you our greetings and our power from the Center. Lutbunn."

February 22, 1952.

"I am Elcar, 6th projection, 42nd wave, 4th sector patrol, realms of Schare. I forward to you our congratulations from our central control. You shall be seeing much more of us. Elcar. Discontinue.

* * *

These first three messages were efforts to become accustomed to this powerful vibration.

March 7, 1952.

"Greetings from the realms of Schare. Watch your skies in your months of May to August. I am Clota, 9th projection, 2nd wave, planet patrol, realms of Schare. Discontinue.

* * *

This message was given in March and in the months of May to August, more saucers were seen than ever before, including those over Washington, D. C.

March 21, 1952.

"Greetings. I am Totalmon, 4th projection, 7th wave, space patrol, realms of Schare. Elevation 750 miles above you, speed 170,000 miles per second; returning from the 2nd sector. Our light-cast instructs us to bring you blessings from the Center and the realms of Blaau. Discontinue."

April 4, 1952.

"Salutations to you beings in the 12th realm of the 3rd sector. My instructions are to transmit to you the clearance, authority and blessings from the Center of Schare. We have recently placed 7000 additional units in the patrol of this system. These will be reinforced in the very near future. I am Latamarx, 62nd projection, 5th wave, planet patrol, realms of Schare. Discontinue."

* * *

The above two messages were more to accomplish the contact and effect an improvement in attunement.

April 6th, 1952.

"May I greet you in peace. I am Noma, from the Central Command, 64th projection, 7th wave, 4th sector patrol, realms of Schare. My authority permits me to give you certain information. *Your pentagon will soon have much to muddle over. We are going to give this globe a buzz. I hope they do not intercept us from in front.* Our authority has ordered us to maintain contact through you. When we are ready, we shall do some intercepting also, and we shall also land when we are ready. Our Central Circle sends their blessings. Discontinue."

* * *

This message received in April was carried out three months later in the latter part of July. The pentagon, can only mean Washington, D. C. There is no doubt they had "much to muddle over." The "buzz" was accomplished by the saucer beings. The statement that the saucers hoped the Air Force would not intercept them in front, indicates that the saucers also knew in advance that there would be an attempt to intercept them. Is it coincidence that a letter mailed by me to Air Forces Intelligence Command, at the request of the Saucer beings in the July 18th message, was in their hands when the "buzz" occurred? I do not comprehend how the letter's arrival, the "buzz," the reference to the pentagon, and the expected interception, can all be coincidence. My belief is that the saucer beings timed it that way, to let the Air Force know that this information was authentic. Their return receipt showed they received the letter July 22, 1952. The "buzz" was on July 26, 27 and 28th.

April 11, 1952.

"Greetings. My identity is Leektow, 51st projection, 7th wave, realms of Schare. Your globe will be effected by the death of one of the highest leaders causing great strife. Discontinue."

"I am Luu, 61st projection, 7th wave, 3rd sector patrol, realms of Schare. I am instructed to inform you that Leektow's transmission was interrupted by ionized particles and extreme distance above these nebulous clouds. Discontinue."

* * *

As far as I know this prophecy has not yet been fulfilled.

April 12, 1952.

"Greetings. I am Oblow, 62nd projection, 7th wave, 3rd sector patrol, realms of Schare. I am instructed to inform you that the mortal beings of this planet have *nothing to fear* from the beings of Schare. When we come, we shall come in peace. Any interference will be obliterated and opposition useless. We have no reason to destroy. Countless eons of time, through cycles past we forgot that destruction was of any use. Discontinue."

* * *

This message expresses "peaceful" intent on the part of the saucer beings. Their advanced development can be seen in the last sentence.

April 19, 1952.

"Greetings. I am Kerrull, 64th projection, 2nd wave, 4th sector patrol, realms of Schare. We are now at the planet you call Mars. We shall proceed to your planet leveling off some 700 miles above the surface. We are instructed from the center to inform you that due to inaccurate calculations, many of your fellow beings will *suffer prolonged illness* from an experiment to be conducted next week. This folly in the use of atomic power for destruction will rebound upon the users. Discontinue."

* * *

This message can be verified by medical science. Newspapers have carried articles signifying a rapid increase in pernicious anemia. This message was received several days prior to atomic bomb tests near Las Vegas, Nevada.

April 25, 1952.

"I am Locktopar, 21st projection, 16th wave, 3rd sector patrol, realms of Schare. My instructions are to transmit our greetings and blessings from the Center of Blaau. Your free press does not reveal to you that we have been sighted numerous times; neither does it inform you of the disastrous effect of this last play with universal substance. Soon we shall inform you ourselves. Discontinue."

* * *

This message explains itself.

April 27, 1952.

"Greetings. I am Molca, 22nd projection, 3rd wave, 4th sector patrol, realms of Schare. We have been directed to advance you certain information from our Center. We are stationary 72 miles above your location. Your contact is aboard. Do not be confused between what you call fireballs, flying saucers and cigar shaped objects all seen by your people. Those cigar shaped ships are space ships from a neighboring planet and as you know, the fireballs are ships from Blaau. Our so-called saucers are from Schare. There are three separate checks being made upon this globe at present. Some of the cigar-shaped ships are not investigating with peaceful intent and our investigation concerns them as much as this globe. We shall keep a close watch upon them and they know it. Now that your curious one has bounced around here a while we shall inform you that our ships travel by polarized light direction. Your so-called magnetism is one form of light direction. Now he has discovered our cross-grain construction through which we maintain direction. We return your contact before he discovers how to create our ships. Discontinue."

* * *

The above message tells us that their energy is polarized light direction. It also says, that we refer to their power as magnetism.

May 2, 1952.

"Greetings. I am Clatu, 2nd projection, 4th wave, 3rd sector patrol, realms of Schare. Are you prepared for us to alight? We know the orders are to destroy us, shoot us down if necessary to discover how we are made. I am instructed to inform you we cannot be shot down. Your pentagon recently arrived at a conclusion that we are of a higher intelligence; they did not decide, however, that we also are of a higher authority! They will decide, that in the very near future. In your next four months, commencing now, watch the skies, look to the East. Rest assured, when we descend we will not be able to carry on a personal conversation with most of those in official capacity. We shall land. Discontinue."

* * *

This message explains itself.

May 9, 1952.
"Salutations. I am Hulda. Senior in command, 11th projection, 7th wave, realms of Schare. I am instructed to inform you that the beings of the 4th sector, Blaau, are returning. Your people shall witness more fireballs. Discontinue."

* * *

After this message, fireballs were witnessed over the northwestern states of the United States. The saucer beings' reference to Blaau is the name they give to the sector of the universe that our solar system is now moving into.

May 16, 1952.

"Salutations. I am identified as Lata, fleet commander, 40th projection, 7th wave, realms of Schare. Be it known to you that we are combining our efforts to reach an attunement that will permit us to transmit from Blaau through the Council of the *Seven Lights* to you beings here and vice versa. Our fleet is standing by to complete this contact. Discontinue."

* * *

This message explains that the saucer beings were assisting us, in our meeting, to reach another vibratory attunement through our regular contact center, The Council of the Seven Lights.

May 17, 1952.

"Hail, fortunate ones. I am Singba, regional fleet authority for the entire 45th projection, all waves, realms of Schare. I am instructed to tell you that the Center Blaau, Schare and multitudes of other Centers too numerous to mention are rejoicing tonight in honor of the contacts that were made with your group last night. As a reward, my Center has given me authority to describe vaguely this ship I command. In your dimensions my, what you would call flagship, is 300 feet thick and 1500 feet in diameter. Our crew 7200. Oh, they're not crowded, don't forget, *they don't have to go around each other. Neither do our ships.* Our propulsion is the transmutation of hard light particles into soft light particles. Let your scientists figure that one out. Not being fourth dimensional minded they will discount any possibility of such a thing. Let me inform you further light does not travel. Light is. The transmutation of energy through intelligent direction causes each cosmic particle to hand this energy called light from one atom to the next. There is no movement and that which does not move, does not travel. Our ships are composed of light substance, indestructible in the material sense, though we can arrive where we have no further use for the ship and discharge the atoms composing it. Your few smart men of science are guessing up this alley now. This has been a pleasure and I hope to return in the near future. Discontinue."

* * *

In this message the beings from Schare (Share-ee) indicate that both themselves and their saucers are composed of light substance. They can cross through each other, like the beams from two flashlights, without disturbance.

May 23, 1952.
"Greetings. I am Kletarc, 42nd projection, 3rd wave, realms of Schare. In answer to your vibration requesting tomorrow's news. A world famous woman will be involved in a controversy that will lead to international conflict. This nation shall reach a crisis period in your month of September. July will see new aggression in the Far East. We are about to pass out of your cone of receptivity, 72,148.2 miles above you. Discontinue."

May 30, 1952.
"Greetings. I am Rouee, 45th vibration, authority 7th wave, realms of Schare. My center has instructed

me to notify you that our power and our blessings are being attuned to assist you to reach this vibratory level necessary to cross the border. Discontinue."

June 1, 1952.

"I greet you in love. I am Blorah, executive authority, all vibrations projected from all waves, 3rd sector from Schare. My instructions are to inform you that the center of the quadra sector, Blaau, and the combined beings of the 4th sector send you congratulations for making direct contact through the arc. Our station, Schare, also advances through me congratulations. Discontinue."

June 11, 1952.

"Salutations. I am Kleac, 5th projection, 7th wave, realms of Schare. I am instructed to inform you that your month of July shall see much blood shed. Discontinue."

June 13, 1952.

"Greetings. I am Tonla, ranking authority, 72nd projection, 16th wave, realms of Schare. We have been interested in your earlier discussion. We ignore it. Our purpose is not announced to anyone. My entire fleet projection has been attuned so that radion projections will assist you in your reception from Uni. Discontinue."

June 14, 1952.

"Greetings. I am Tolta, 11th projection, 7th wave realms of Schare. In the coming week one of the rogues occupying a high governmental office shall be stricken fatally. Discontinue."

June 28, 1952.

"Salutations. My identity is Qel, 72nd projection, 15th wave, realms of Schare. We are passing over your cone of receptivity, 172 thousand miles above you. Our center requests that I inform you. You will see more of us if you watch the skies. Discontinue."

June 29, 1952.

"Greetings. I am Rea, 7th projection, 21st wave, realms of Schare. I am authorized to inform you we are now crossing your state of Texas, at 70 thousand feet and will pass over your cone of receptivity in a few minutes. Discontinue."

* * *

Several of our members witnessed this display of light control. Two luminous streaks in the sky were visible overhead. These light streaks disappeared over their entire length, simultaneously and instantly, as though a light switch had been turned off.

July 3, 1952.

"Greetings, thou mortal being of Shan. I am Klacta, 6000th projection, all waves authority, realms of Schare. I am instructed to inform you that you are about to witness the most unpredictable weather you have ever seen, in the immediate future. Discontinue."

This is verified by numerous crop failures later. There have also been weather extremes since July.

July 4, 1952.

"Greetings. I am Betth, 176th projection, 67th wave, realms of Schare. Our center requests that I inform you to *be prepared for a good earth shake*. Discontinue."

* * *

Proof that the saucer beings from the station Schare not only know what is happening, but also what is going to happen, is verified by this reception, It happened 17 days later in Tehachapi and continued through Bakersfield, California.

July 6, 1952.

"Salutations. My identity is Dulac, 411th projection, authority all waves, realms of Schare. Our center has directed me to throw the combined power of all waves under my authority to ray you a substance that will be very advantageous to your mortal being, your physical body. We are standing by 4300 miles above you, 742 in this projection. Our ray is now directed to you. Discontinue."

* * *

Following this message all those members present at this meeting, about 23, felt the same fluid sensation, like a warm fluid being run over their bodies.

July 18, 1952.

"Greetings. I am Portla, 712th projection, 16th wave, realms of Schare. Approaching your solar system is a ventla with our chief aboard, commandant of the station Schare in charge of the first four sectors. His vehicle will be over your center very shortly. In the meantime we have rayed you the substance for your better reception. We are waiting here at 72,000 miles above you to welcome our chief, *who will be entering this solar system for the first time*. He will inform you of the purpose of your organization through the direct inspiration of Schonling, Saochane, the Council of the Twelve Lords and the Council of the Seven Lights. Discontinue."

* * *

Hail to you beings of Shan. I greet you in love and peace. My identity is Ashtar, commandant quadra sector, patrol station Schare, all projections, all waves. Greetings. Through the Council of the Seven Lights you have been brought here, inspired with the inner light to help your fellow man. You are mortals, and other mortals can only understand that which their fellow man can understand. The purpose of this organization is, in a sense, to save mankind from himself. Some years ago, your time, your nuclear physicists penetrated the "Book of Knowledge." They discovered how to explode the atom. Disgusting as the results have been, that this force should be used for destruction, it is not compared to that which can be. We have *not* been concerned with their explosion of plutonium and U235, the Uranium mother element; this atom is an *inert* element.

"We are concerned, however, with their attempt to explode the hydrogen element. This element is *life giving* along with five other elements in the air you breathe, in the water you drink, in the composition of your physical self. In much of your material planet is this *life giving* atomic substance, *hydrogen*. Their efforts in the field of science have been successful to the extent that they are not content to rest on the laurels of a power beyond their use; not content with the entire destruction of an entire city at a time. They must have something more destructive. They've got it. When they explode the hydrogen atom, they shall extinguish life on this planet. They are *tinkering with a formula they do not comprehend*. They are destroying a life-giving element of the Creative Intelligence. Our message to you is this: You shall advance to your government all information we have transmitted to you. You shall request that your government shall immediately contact all other earth nations regardless of political feelings. Many of your physicists with an inner perception development have refused to have anything to do with the explosion of the hydrogen atom. The explosion of an atom of *inert* substance and that of a *living* substance are two different things. We are not concerned with man's desire to continue war on this planet, Shan. We are concerned with their deliberate determination to *extinguish humanity* and turn this planet into a cinder.

"Your materialists will disagree with our attempt to warn mankind. Rest assured they shall cease to explode *life giving* atoms, or we shall eliminate all projects connected with such. Our missions are peaceful, but this condition occurred before in this solar system and the planet Lucifer was torn to bits. We are determined that it shall not happen again. The governments on the planet Shan have conceded that we are of a higher intelligence. *They must concede also that we are of a higher authority.* We do not have to enter their buildings to know what they are doing. We have the formula they would like to use. It is not meant for destruction. Your purpose here has been to build a receptivity that we could communicate with your planet, for by the attraction of light substance atoms, we patrol your universe.

"To your government and to your people and through them to all governments and all peoples on the planet of Shan, accept the warning as a blessing that mankind may survive. My light, we shall remain in touch here at this cone of receptivity. My love, I am Ashtar."

* * *

This July 18th message explains the purpose of the saucers in the skies of our planet. There is no doubt that everyone, in *all* the nations on this planet, *knows* within their reasoning that the Hydrogen Bomb is a vicious evil means of taking the Creator's power of life into the hands of man. Science teaches us that for every action there is a reaction. This isn't man made law, this is universal law. By creating destruction, on an ever increasing scale, man is causing the action. We are not interested in what these minorities do, who determine to spend the money of the multitudes for progress. How far in the darkness of ignorance can they be to kill off the "geese" that lay their "golden eggs?" Do they expect to avoid the reaction?

July 25, 1952.

"Salutations. My identity is Maxslow, 6032nd projection, 74th wave, realms of Schare. We are at 170,000 feet above this cone of receptivity. I am instructed to inform you that your letters of information have caused numerous materialists to stop and think for the first time in their mortal existence. I am further instructed to inform you that our center has reinforced the patrol in this system of Salon with an additional 42,000 projections. Discontinue."

August 1, 1952.

"In the light of universal law, I greet you in peace. I am Ashtar. With reference to all attempts to trap us, I would suggest that it would be much easier to trap a character off the visor of your television. When your authorities discover how to trap light substance, we would also like to know the formula. We ignore any further discussion of this subject.

"Our efforts are in the cause of peace, true peace. Many of your higher authorities throughout the nations of the planet Shan have lost all comprehension of the word peace, for they are under the influences of the forces of darkness. The first thought that enters the minds of those in this darkness is not to find out what *the other object of our visitation is,* but rather to destroy us, to find out what we are made of. We can assure you that all their efforts, made with the object of destruction, will avail them naught. Those individuals assigned to the station of Schare are capable of conversing through mental telepathy with mortal beings in the higher light on the planet Shan, at will. We are not desirous of staging a show but I will inform you that if opposition forces, mortal or otherwise, persist in their efforts we can put 100,000 units a second in operation. They will be financially embarrassed to produce mechanical aircraft at that rate. For those few whose mentality is not diverted—men of science —I shall inform you that our ships could not be visible to the mortal eye of the people of Shan were it not for the elements in your atmosphere. A few enlightened minds will understand that. It is difficult to make one reason who has lost all reason. It is difficult for any mortal to conceive of higher intelligence in various stages, they have been away from it so long. I would also inform your government of this nation that the information that was mailed to the Intelligence, was transmitted to foreign nations out of their own office. In the light of a peace beyond the comprehension of mortal beings, we shall remain with you. I am Ashtar, commandant, station Schare."

August 3, 1952.

"Salutations. I am Lax, 9400th projection, 604th wave, realms of Schare. I am instructed to inform you that your material-minded mortals shall be convinced. Discontinue."

August 8, 1952.

"I am Blaroc, assistant to Ashtar, all projections, all waves, station of Schare. Much of the information we could advance to you from our center is being withheld due to a law of security measure in your nation which could place you within the penalty of treason. We are not going to give you information that will endanger you.

"You are advised from our center to especially observe the skies for your period of the next few weeks. There will be an earthquake in your southern hemisphere in the immediate future. Discontinue."

August 10, 1952.

"The light and blessings of Schare are transmitted to you and from our center. We are instructed to advance to you their blessings. I am Blaroc. You have my official status recorded. Our center requests that I advance you this information. Our projections are about to be witnessed by many of the people throughout all the countries of this planet over several of your most important cities. When the governments decide that they shall abandon their development of nuclear destruction through the use of the element hydrogen, we shall then inform them of *the other object* of our interest in this planet Shan. Our perception of what is going on has not created the faintest concern among our higher authorities. We can see the purpose of hidden control. We can also foresee its failure in the future. Discontinue."

August 15, 1952.

"Greetings, thou being of Shan. In the light of love and peace I come to you. Commandant of the station Schare. I am Ashtar. Having returned to the station Schare from the center, I advance to your scientists the following information.

"We have told you that the element hydrogen is a living substance. In the composition of your physical being, in the air you breathe, in the water you drink, are five elements of living substance besides hydrogen—the elements nitrogen, oxygen, carbon, flourine and sodium. Much of your material science has been directed to disproving theory that does not conform to the personal beliefs of some scientific authority. Among the scientific mentalities of this planet, Shan, are many minor scientists, who do not have the authority to change these opinions that have been disproved. We have advanced you information in the faint hope that some of your governmental authorities would grasp the fact that with the explosion of living substance they create a condition parallel to what your scientists call frozen equilibrium. This release of free hydrogen into the atmosphere of this planet will cause flames to engulf many portions of this planet momentarily. Those in authority in the governments are assuming direct responsibility, not only for the people inhabiting this planet, but their own immediate families, wives, children, parents and relatives are also their responsibility, for these dear ones shall not escape. You in authority, of the governments of the planet Shan, think twice if you would have your loved ones with you. Consult your physicists. Ask them about the parallel condition of frozen equilibrium. They will inform you, if they speak the truth and are not influenced otherwise by the forces of darkness, that this is truth.

"Wake up, you who would believe only those who direct you. Stand before the people. Tell those who influence your mental decisions that they too are involved. In the light of love, I transmit you a continuous beam here, through a ventla which has been stationed in this cone of receptivity at a level 72,000 miles above you, beyond reach of any traps. I shall return, my love. I am Ashtar."

August 17, 1952.

"Greetings. I am identified as Noot, stationed in the ventla within the cone of your receptivity. I am from the 7000th projection, 11th wave. My instructions are to transmit to you that substance beam for your better inner perception. This light transmission on a vibration level above the ultra violet is being rayed to you continuously. You may become more perceptive to the feeling of this substance anytime you gather here. (Other than when you are receiving projections from Lem and Cor.) You only have to join hands to receive this substance vibration. Discontinue."

August 22, 1952.

"From the sector system of Vela, I greet you from the quadra sector station Schare, in love and peace. I am Ashtar, commandant, all projections, all waves. We have transmitted to you numerous messages and requested that they be forwarded to your government, and through them to all governments of this planet Shan. This transcript tonight is not for your government. You who have devoted your efforts to attaining to this receptivity are entitled to some information for yourselves. We are not desirous of creating any further confusion on this planet. You are to make every immediate effort to consolidate this center. Many brothers are being inspired to join you here. You are instructed to work together without personal regard for individual property. You are instructed further to consolidate your unity to build all structures possible to prepare for immediate changes, especially prepare for food storage due to rapid changes now affecting the financial, military and political conjunction. We advance you this information in the light of true love. I am Ashtar."

August 24, 1952.

"In the love and peace of eternal light, greetings to the mortal beings of Shan. I am Ashtar. Let me first inform you that we are grateful for your continual efforts in maintaining this contact power.

"For the information of your scientific minds throughout the planet, Shan, our ventlas do not spin. The emanation of spiral radiation from our ships gives the illusion of spinning. The upper or positive polarity of a ventla radiates emanations outwardly from the center. Due to the collection and concentration of light particles through a vortice funnel in the center unseen, these light emanations radiating outward appear as grooves on one of your phonograph records. The lower negative polarity operates in a reverse manner. This light substance emanation is contained within a field of zero circumference which is void giving, the impression of an edge. Your spectroscopic camera will reveal us only as light in the spectrum, plus elements in your atmosphere. Advance this information also to those who still doubt. I leave you with love. I am Ashtar."

August 31, 1952.

"I am Ashtar, in the process of attempting to straighten out numerous conditions that affect this planet Shan. We are going to give you certain information, in the future, that will weld together the two great sciences of your people. I refer to all branches of material science and religion. These two are one in truth, separated only by a gap that we shall give you the key to close.

"In the quadra sector Blaau, man on the planet Shan will have no further use for the misconception, that he is faced with in the form of religion, for science of truth, seen and unseen, is the basis of religion, not ancient scriptures, misinterpreted, mistranslated and misconstrued by those who deliver lectures, but based on the true science of life in all phases. Organized scientists are beginning now to explore these realms of the unseen. My love, I am Ashtar."

Sept. 12, 1952.

"In the light of all lights, I extend you blessings from our Center. I am Ashtar. Our Center has requested that I advance to you mortal beings of Shan the following information. Over your past several months our ventlas have discharged several thousand light beings in certain remote areas upon your planet. These individuals, serving the cause of universal law, are recording numerous occurrences taking place within the civilization of the people of Shan. It would be advisable to instruct any mortal being who by chance should approach any of our light intelligences to do so with a thought projection of peace, "I am friendly." Any approach in any other frame of thought will meet with instant defensive conditions. It is not our desire to injure anyone. Only under individual protective measures shall we do anything other than retreat. In the records obtained by these beings from Schare, we shall determine what action to take in the very near future.

Our center requests that I advance you congratulations and thanks for maintaining this contact. My love remains with you. I am Ashtar."

Sept. 21, 1952.

"In love and peace, I am with you. I am Ashtar, commandant quadra sector station, Schare. We are about to add further confusion to the minds of those who are attempting to diagnose our existence. We are about to be sighted under the surface of the water at many points throughout the oceans of Shan. You have been given sufficient evidence through the recent storm in your Pacific Ocean, through verification of much information advanced to you by us. My perception is that most of you within this cone have accepted us through proof. All future demonstrations on our part will establish us in the minds of the majority of those doubters throughout this planet Shan. I leave you with my love. I am Ashtar."

Oct. 3, 1952.

"I greet you in love and peace. I am Ashtar, commandant vela quadra sector station, Schare. Blessings. We are highly gratified to know that the limited minds of mortals in authority of the planet Shan are beginning to get a faint understanding of our true being. In the future we shall appear visible at different attitudes in different altitudes in different forms and colors at different speeds and stationary, both of densities perceptible to your electronics and imperceptible. Within the atmosphere of Shan our manipulations of light substance can be reflected so that we are not where we appear to be. Those individual beings from Schare now on your planet are being instructed to transmit certain carrier frequencies that will cause a variety of conditions to be apparent in your many varieties of electronic receivers. My love. I am Ashtar."

Panoramic ground photo of Death Valley

Since the printing of the first edition of this book the following messages have been received from the saucer beings:

Oct. 17, 1952.

"I am Ashtar. The suppression of your free press has prevented the beings of Shan from knowing that we have been sighted numerous times, under very peculiar circumstances. This same restricting force is withholding from your people certain vital information regarding extreme magnetic changes accelerating the declination line with increasing rapidity. Your top Air Force officials are about to reveal a few authentic deductions, mingled with comic book fantasy. No authority on Shan can withhold the power of our arrival when we mean business, for then your skies will be lighted at night by several million of us. I extend our gratification to you, from our center, for maintaining this contact. My love, Ashtar. Discontinue."

* * *

It is common knowledge that the reading public is not informed of many things until months or years afterward. Many officials in governments have appointed themselves as judges, to determine what the public should be informed of, "for their own good," "for national security," or some other reason.

It has recently been disclosed that about 47,000 men have deserted from our armed forces. Did this happen all at once? If not, why was it being withheld from the people?

If our active and reserve military forces have 47,000 deserters in a few million, can one assume that the same ratios of civilians have "mentally deserted" from the ranks of our total population, for the same reason?

Why are our casualty lists being withheld? Is this still a government of the people and by the people, or has the adult public been classed as "children who shouldn't be informed of the facts of life" for some other obscure reason, determined by those who are elected to represent us?

"Thou shalt not kill" is universal law and though the author does not condone desertion, it should be apparent, to the officials of all governments, that a change in *thinking* is occurring in the *minds* of *many,* who are aware that the "signs in the skies" mean *something*.

It is apparent that the agents of universal law, the beings of the ventlas, *know* what is being done. The recent demonstration over Dallas, Texas, should convince many that conditions are about to be changed.

Since man first started recording signs and symbols an arrow or spear pointing has indicated the *right way*. We today can see on any road sign this same symbol.

In the ancient records, an arrow meant *spirit,* or a *higher realm* of intelligent beings. (Refer to page 604 of Oahspe).

The arrow seen in the sky over Dallas, Texas, is verification of the October 3rd message, and a revelation of proof, that the *Spirit* of *Christ Consciousness* is returning.

November 14, 1952.

"In the light of love and peace, I am with you. I am Ashtar. Despite recent misinformation disseminated among the people of the planet Shan, the explosion reported to the people of your country is false in part. We are withholding certain information for a specific reason; however, we shall inform you that an *isotope* is not an *atomic element*. I am Ashtar. Discontinue."

* * *

This message was received three days after newspapers carried large headlines announcing that the hydrogen bomb had been exploded. Later the same papers carried statements, by top physicists, that the explosion was *not* the hydrogen bomb. The official government explanation was that it was a "nuclear device."

November 23, 1952.

"Greetings in the light of peace. I am Ashtar, commandant quadra sector, station Schare. Let me inform you man's efforts to conquer space are limited to the satalite, the moon. Any attempt by man to extend space flight beyond the earths' vortice will end any possibility of returning to Shan, the earth. We are now passing through the orbit ring known to you as the 7th Light. I am authorized from our center to inform you this orbit of Uni is known and identified in the unseen realms as the ring of Mas. I, Ashtar, return your contact to the Council of the Seven Lights on Shanchea. Discontinue."

* * *

This message does not explain why man cannot extend space flights beyond the moon, to other planets. It is probable that our lack of knowledge about conditions in space does not permit us to comprehend an explanation of conditions that are not at present a part of our limited space theories.

The planet Uni and the satelite of earth called Shanchea, require lengthy explanations. They are explained fully in the author's forthcoming book entitled "The Council of the Seven Lights."

December 5, 1952.

"I salute you from Schare. I am Ashtar. Our center instructs me to advance to you their deep appreciation for maintaining this contact center in the face of ridicule. Our center also authorizes me to give you the following information.

"By our authority, several hundred of our light intelligences on the planet Shan, have brought about the vibration change that has placed them within physical bodies such as yours. This has been accomplished for a condition that will be revealed to you later. Within the vortice of this planet Shan, we have also established several substations. Our love to you. I am Ashtar."

* * *

This message is self-explanatory.

January 11, 1953.

"In the Light of love and peace. I am Ashtar. You will be observing an increasing variety of signs in the skies. We are having difficulty with this attunement. Prepare for extreme cold. My love. I am Ashtar."

* * *

This message was followed two weeks later by extremely cold weather.

January 23, 1953.

"I am Ashtar, commandant Vela quadra sector, station Schare. As we have informed you, our center has authorized three sub-stations within the vortice of your planet Shan. Each of these stations now are in a position to release five hundred thousand ventlas each. Our center instructs me to inform you that you are once again about to see the use of atomic weapons in warfare. I am further requested to extend our gratitude to you for maintaining this contact vibration. In the Light of true love and peace. I am Ashtar. Discontinue."

February 13, 1953.

"Hail in love and peace. I am Ashtar, commandant Vela quadra sector, station Schare. You have just heard the authority granted by Schonling, Lord God of the third dimensional sector, for our authority to take corrective measures. We are creating a Light energy vortice near the planet Shan in an effort to stabilize your planet. This effort requires the combined forces of 86 projections, 9100 waves, of 236,000 ventlas. Needless to say this vortice is going to create extensive damage to counteract the unbalance man has created on Shan. Our center extends to you their love and blessings. My Light. I am Ashtar."

February 27, 1953.

"Greetings in love and peace. I am Ashtar, Vela quadra sector, station Schare, commandant. We wish to instruct you to prepare for violent disturbances on Shan. We are having our first indications of success in arresting the attitude of Shan. My love. I am Ashtar. Discontinue."

March 6, 1953.

"Greetings in the Light of love and peace. I am Ashtar, commandant, Vela quadra sector, station Schare. Our survey of the solar system of Salon indicates that the other planets of this system have not been affected by the actions of the people of the planet Shan. You will continue to witness very unusual weather conditions. Many of the ventlas from the sub-stations established near your planet will become very active in your atmosphere in your months of April to September. I am asked to advance gratitude and congratulations through to you from our center. My Light and my love, Ashtar. Discontinue."

March 13, 1953.

"Hail in love and peace, O beings of Shan. I am Ashtar, commandant Vela quadra sector, station Schare. Our center requests that I extend to you their grateful appreciation for maintaining this contact center. Our three sub-stations, located around your planet, are instructed to take an active part in occurrences of violence that are about to occur on your planet. Verification of another of pre-warnings will occur within your next thirty days. My love, Ashtar. Discontinue."

March 20, 1953.

"In love and peace. I am Ashtar. I extend through to you from our center the love and blessings for the service you have extended in maintaining this contact. I am authorized to inform you, we are in constant communication with our people we have in your national capitol. You will be hearing of an increase of phenomena resulting in many hallucinations, so-called, by your people. We have been in your immediate vicinity. I repeat. Do not be alarmed by unusual occurrences around you. We are now over your Mississippi River and now we arrive over your city of San Francisco. It is not our purpose to bring you continual reports of destruction ahead. Man has created his own destructive reaction. Shan is in a terrible state. From our center we have activated three and one-half million primary units around this planet. Our plans are taking shape. Be prepared for anything. My love. I am Ashtar. Discontinue."

* * *

The author would be pleased to know that the readers of this book spend some time watching the skies, especially at night. If you do not see a "saucer" you will discover many other things that will be revealed within your consciousness.

IN CONCLUSION

The foregoing messages need no explanation, except to be interpreted by science.

It can plainly be seen, by anyone of average intelligence, that the saucer beings are here for a purpose. It can also be seen that they are not to be feared.

Man can see, from the ruins of other civilizations on this earth, that reaction is the cataclysmic balance, through universal law, for wrong action.

All the confusion, fear, inflation, war and hatred, have been built through several generations to a point where it is concentrated in atomic bombs, to kill innocent millions.

The *unseen intelligence* is taking a part in balancing an unbalanced condition.

By what *right* does mankind on this planet assume to believe that in all the perfect precision of this boundless universe, man alone is intelligent? Man could be in the same stage—to other intelligences— that insects are to us on this earth.

Certainly it is rank stupidity to believe that the whole universe includes only our planet as the only place that is occupied.

Science continually disproves its own theories. This is the only gauge by which man can record progress. Even time is only recognized as it passes and events recorded *after* they happen. Man accepts three dimensional theory, because the illusion is understandable to his *limited* thinking. With applied, undisturbed effort, man can develop his *all*-dimensional *sense of being,* and record time and events in the future, as well as present and past.

I include here one of our other receptions that has no direct connection with the 'flying saucers" but permits one to realize the *illusion* of this *mortal reflection* called intelligence.

"I gather here from eons past those records written in the flame of eternal truth and from the future yet to come. I gather events today, not to place them on the altar to be sacrificed to needless thought, neither to be scattered in the winds that they may bring to birth another time. Only has the future and the past been gathered for today, that you may be aware that yesterday is tomorrow to many, while yet tomorrow is yesterday to some. For time is effaced by eternity, only to be trampled in the dust of material things, and those who gather stars within the image of themselves, have gathered more than intellects throughout recorded time, for *thought* is not *intelligence*. It is bounded on all sides by opinions expressed by others; too, it will fail you when you need it most. For thought is but the *means* to contact that infallible Ever Presence, the vibration true to all and each, nor rank nor social standing shall it favor. For when man thinks within his day, he sleeps within his night and from his present he gathers words, expressions and actions yet to come. Be not betrayed, for thought alone is only a tiny line of light, connecting true receptivity with inner conscious being. Many events from the past can scar this line and lead you off the path. Remember only light can be eternally the source of all that is."

So the "saucer beings" are here to stay, to direct man back upon the path and prove that theories advanced by science, are only other steps to be disproved, in man's eternal progression to find his true reality. For science is *not* the future; science is the *present* even as history is the past. When man admits to himself his failure, and science accepts the *future* of unseen reality, *true* science will be evident on every hand, in the light of peace and love, rather than in the chaos of war and destruction.

Man only has to *find himself* to realize the tiny part he plays in the cosmic drama called Eternity.

Greet the saucer beings with thoughts of love and receive them as friends, not with "jets" and guns and fear.

I assume full responsibility for being the "contact" for this reception. I do not assume responsibility for others who have used some information they have received at our meetings—that is being published under other titles.

This information from the beings of the Ventlas, from the station Schare, is still being received. Many other contact receptions are to be released soon in a book, "The Council of the Seven Lights."

PANNING IT OUT.

Desert Gold

AN INDIAN WICKIUP.

1st Residents of the American Desert

The Haunted Desert
by Cactus Jim

She was a frail woman, dressed all in white, a look of sadness in her eyes that left you feeling cold and alone. In her wedding gown, she paced the adobe floor of the Vallecito Station patiently waiting for the next stage, which would take her on to Sacramento. Her fiancé had struck it rich in the gold fields and had sent for her to join him in California.

Vallecito Stage Station

She had arrived at the Vallecito Station sometime in the late 1850's and she had never left. The bride had become deathly ill during her journey and died at Vallecito Station. She was buried in an unmarked grave at Campo Santo, a few hundred yards from the station. It is said that if you camp near the old Vallecito Stage Station, you too will see "The Lady In White" restlessly pace the worn earth where the station once stood, waiting for her stage to come.

It is no wonder that so many ghosts haunt the lonely trails, mountains, and landmarks of the forbidding desert. The desert can be so unforgiving and, at the same time, unbelievably generous. Many travelers, prospectors and adventures have gone into the desert, never to return or be seen again. Others have returned with gold nuggets and treasures so rare and unique that we could only dream of being so lucky ourselves.

Unmarked grave at Campo Santo

Desert lore, stories and quests for loot and gold have made men greedy. Gun fights, murders, and death from starvation and dehydration have left many dead on the barren desert trails. Their ghosts still walk the mountain ridges, gullies, and deserted locations they once traveled or lived, spirits with unfinished business, who cannot rest.

Some guard buried treasures and lost mines, while others battle perpetually until death, forever replaying their last moments of life.

The Phantom Stage of Carrizo

The Lady in White is not the only ghost story attached to the Vallecito Stage Station. Not far from Vallecito is Carrizo Wash where the Phantom Stage forges it way through the deep sand, pulled by a team of four mules on moonlit nights. The Phantom Stage is driven by a lone driver hunched over as if asleep. No passengers are seen in the Stage when it passes through Carrizo Wash, hesitating for only a moment, as if planning to stop at the place where the Carrizo Station once stood, but is now only a pile of mud. The Phantom Stage continues on past the old station until out of sight. In the morning one may think twice about actually seeing the Phantom Stage, until he sees the ruts carved from wagon wheels and hoof prints left behind by the ghostly stage that travels by on occasion, as if to keep the trail alive.

No passengers on the Stage

There is another story that coincides with the Phantom Stage. In the 1860s, before the stage line closed, a special stage set out from El Paso headed for San Diego with a box of coins. The stage that carried the coins had one driver and a guard. When the stage reached Yuma, Arizona, the guard fell ill and the driver continued on without him. That same stage was held up by robbers somewhere in the area where the route meanders into Carrizo Wash between the Fish and Coyote Mountains. The driver was shot during the robbery and the thieves stashed the coins on the south slope of Fish Mountain. The coins remain there to this day, they say, because there were too many soldiers passing by on the trail. It is said that after the robbery, the dead driver and the stage continued through Carrizo toward Vallecito Station, but the stage disappeared, never to be seen again.

The White Horse Ghost of Vallecito

Vallecito is famous for its ghosts. Its history contains many murders, deaths, robberies, and other wicked tales. One well known story involves a double-murder at Vallecito Station. It all started with a stage hold up that yielded $65,000 worth of loot to four men on horseback, who robbed the eastbound stage before it reached Carrizo Wash en route to Vallecito Station.

As the men fled the scene, the driver of the stage fired one shot, killing one of the four men. When he reached the thief he had shot, he found not one, but two dead bodies. The driver concluded that the leader of the band of thieves, had shot one of his own men so he would not have to divide up the loot.

The bandit leader and one other thief survived the robbery and rode on to rest at Vallecito Station. Shortly before they arrived at the station, they buried their loot in some nearby hills and rode on to the station for a drink and some food. It is said that the two bandits were arguing while having a drink in the station. One of the bandits, the leader, went outside to check on his horse promising to continue the discussion when he returned. He did return to the station, entering through the doorway mounted on his big white horse, and shot his companion.

As the wounded bandit was dying, he drew his gun and fired back at the leader, killing him dead from the back of his brave white mount. The white horse, spooked by the gun fire and death of his master, ran off into the hills. It is said that when someone is in the valley around midnight, near the location where the bandits buried their loot, the ghost of a White Horse will appear from nowhere, galloping through the sand and then disappearing without a trace.

The Ghost Lights of Borrego

Anza-Borrego Desert State Park and the Borrego Springs area of California are notorious for the many legends, ghost stories and unexplained phenomena occurring there over the years. The region of the Sonoran Desert is home to the Vallecito Stage Station, Yaqui Well, in addition to the mysterious "Ghost Lights" of Oriflamme Mountain.

The first account of the "Phantom Lights" of Borrego was reported in 1858 by a Butterfield Stage driver. Since then soldiers, prospectors and explorers have reported seeing similar lights. The sightings have been reported near Oriflamme Mountain, over Borrego Valley and in other nearby areas. The occurrences are always slightly different, but the general description of the sightings is the same.

In 1892, a prospector by the name of Charles Knowles and two other men were camping near Grapevine Canyon at the entrance to the Narrows, where they reported their sighting of "Fire Balls." Knowles described the "lights" as balls of fire that rose up approximately 100 feet in the air and then exploded. Knowles compared the "Fire Balls" to fireworks. He saw three "Fire Balls" rise and cascade upon explosion, before they stopped. About 30 minutes later the "Lights" started again, but this time they were different. The "lights" rose into an arch pattern returning to the ground without exploding. The "Light" would then reverse itself and go back to the place where it started.

Oriflamme Mountain.

Scientists have tried to determine a logical explanation for the "Ghost lights." One scientific explanation suggests that when the wind blows sand against quartz outcroppings, static electricity is created, which could look like bright lights or sparks on a dark night.

Some believe that the lights were signals used by bootleggers during prohibition or US Immigration for smuggling operations related to the Mexican Boarder. The only problem with these two explanations is that the sightings had been going on long before and after the time constricted by the events described above.

Another notion is that the "Fire Balls" indicate the location of buried treasure. There are stories that support this latter theory of buried treasure. One of the stories tells of a young man who found many gold nuggets in a gully within the Oriflammes. Another man by the name of George Benton found a boulder of rock, weighing a ton, that contained gold. He found the boulder in the Oriflammes.

The Eight-Foot Skeleton

If you find yourself out late in the desert night, somewhere between the Superstition Mountains and Seventeen Palms, you may see the apparition of an 8-foot skeleton with a lantern in his chest. A prospector by the name of Charley Arizona first saw the ghost about 4 miles southeast of Borrego.

It was a dark night and Charley had already set up camp and was settling down for the night. Not long after Charley turned in for the night, something disturbed his burros and he went to investigate. Suddenly, he saw a large human skeleton with a lantern light shining through its ribs. The skeleton walked in a crazy fashion, as if looking for something or as if it were lost. Shortly after Charley sighted the skeleton, it disappeared over a small ridge.

About two years later, two prospectors had a similar experience while camping in the Superstition Mountains. They caught sight of a flickering light in the distance and wondered what it was; it quickly disappeared. One of the prospectors thought it looked like a skeleton carrying a lantern, but they figured it was the fire reflecting off a rock.

The two prospectors didn't think much of the incident until a year later, when a traveler came into the Vallecito Station with the tale of a skeleton he saw wandering in the desert carrying a light. It wasn't long before news of the skeleton got around and two adventurers went out into the desert to search for this legendary skeleton ghost.

During their third night in the desert, they encountered the ghastly lit skeleton. One of the men shot at it with a gun, but the skeleton continued on unfazed by the gun fire. The two men followed the skeleton for three miles as it wandered in a strange and intermittent gait, over ridges and through valleys, before they lost track of it.

Many believe that the skeleton is the ghost of a prospector who discovered and worked the Phantom mine, which has been lost for many years. The skeleton is no better off than the rest of us, for he too continues to search for the lost Phantom Mine, wandering the dark desert nights looking for his final resting place.

Ghosts Dancers at Yaqui Well

Not far from the Phantom Mine lies another place where skeletons have been seen. During warm summer nights, when the moon is full, ghosts dance at Yaqui Well. The ghosts are said to be the spirits of three emigrants who were traveling from Yuma to California. In search of a shorter route through the desert, the emigrants arrived at Yaqui Well, exhausted and near death from lack of food and water. One of the three travelers drank from the well as much water as he could hold. He died shortly there after. The other two men also drank from the well, but survived.

Yaqui Well

While moving their dead companion's body, the other two noticed some rock specimens that fell out of his pocket. The two men were excited to discover the rocks contained gold, but they did not know where their friend had found the samples. The two men became very excited about the gold and the excitement soon turned into a frenzy of greed and distrust. The two men began to struggle until one finally drowned the other in the muddy water of Yaqui Well.

An Indian watched these events unfold from a nearby hill. The Indian felt it was safe to talk to the one man who had survived, but the emigrant was still so excited as he described his story to the Indian, he entered a state of frenzy and ran off in to the desert yelling "Gold, Gold."

It is only during the hot summer nights of the full moon that the three emigrants return to Yaqui Well. One rises out of the muddy waters of the Yaqui Well, one emerges from the brush nearby, and the third arrives in a cool breeze out of the wash. The ghosts join hands and circle Yaqui

Well in a dance. Soon after the twirling begins, they disappear, leaving only the good waters of the well and a slight chill in the air.

The desert holds many secrets of buried treasures, lost travelers and mysterious sightings. The stories shared with you on these pages are only a small sample of the tales and legends that have been spun for centuries. In the months to follow, DesertUSA Magazine will share more legends of lost mines, tales of buried treasures and more sad stories of heartsick strangers stranded on the desert sands.

Credit www.DesertUSA.com

P.O. Box 270219; San Diego, California 92198-0219
760 740 1787 ext. 1# - Fax 760 546 0321
http://www.dwmi.com

The Mojave Desert is an arid land of wide vistas and sparse vegetation. In the Mojave Mountains area, Pleistocene and Holocene alluvial deposits and Miocene volcanic rocks cover a Proterozoic and Mesozoic crystalline rock basement.

Little Known Spectacular Wonders of the Mojave Desert
Mitchell Caverns and Winding Stair Cave, developed in the Bird Spring Formation of Permian age, are the most important solution caverns known in the Mojave Desert biophysiographic province.

Charlie Manson's Death Valley Daze
by Adam Gorightly

In the Manson Family's brief but eventful history, Charlie and his tribe lived a vagabond existence which led them to several diverse locals across the Golden State, among them the Haight-Ashbury during 67's Summer of Love; later for a period of time at Spahn Ranch near Chatsworth; then lastly, during their final days, Death Valley.

The Manson Family first began hanging out in Death Valley in October of 1968, when a former Buffalo Springfield groupie, Cathy Gillies, hipped Charlie to an abandoned mining claim, Myers Ranch. In time, Myers Ranch became one of a handful of desert outposts where Charlie and his troops would take refuge to escape the envisioned Helter Skelter that Manson saw coming down fast in the form of a black uprising in the cities. Here Charlie would sit out the carnage and once the smoke had cleared, he would then return triumphant to the ruined cities and the blacks would then hand over control to him because they wouldn't know what to do with their new found power. At least this is the version as presented by Vincent Bugliosi as part of his prosecution case depicting Manson as a madman with delusions of grandeur.

The main hub during Manson's Death Valley daze was Barker Ranch, and from that focal point Charlie's Family spread themselves over a vast area which encompassed Goler Wash and the surrounding Panamint Mountains, as they holed up in mining claims throughout the area. During this period, Manson retained a foothold at Spahn Ranch, and began devising a master plan to expedite a mass Manson Family exodus once the shit hit the fan and he needed to move his remaining Family members and dune buggy squadron out of Spahn's and into the desert in a timely manner. To this end, Charlie bought hundreds of dollars worth of topographic maps to chart this planned desert escape route which began behind Spahn Ranch, up into the Santa Susana Mountains by way of Devil's Canyon, then through Simi Valley, bypassing highways, going under culverts, across the Mojave Desert and eventually to Death Valley. This secret route was to be used at the time of Helter Skelter, when everything was going ape-shit in the cities -- and the highways leading out of L.A. would be in gridlock -- an escape route that would be a quick getaway away from the chaos.

According to former Family member Paul Watkins, part of the impetus behind Charlie's growing paranoia during this period was his discovery of the Beatles' White Album, which Manson interpreted as modern day prophecy, and the Fab Four as messengers of the Apocalypse retitled "Helter Skelter." Quoting Revelation chapter 9:

> And the four angels were loosed
>
> Which were prepared for an hour
>
> And a day, and a month, and a year,
>
> For to slay the third part of man
>
> And the fifth angel sounded,
>
> And I saw a star fall from heaven
>
> Unto the earth: and to him was
>
> Given the key to the bottomless pit.

For those with ears to hear, the implications were clear: the four angels were the Beatles, and the fifth angel was Charlie! The "third part of man" was the white race; those who would die in the carnage of Helter Skelter, wiped out for "worship of idols of gold, silver, bronze, stone and wood," (Verse 20) which Charlie related to cars, houses, and money, the modern idols of worship.

The passage, "And he opened the bottomless pit...and there came out of the smoke locusts upon the earth; and unto them was given power as the scorpions of the earth have power" was not only a reference to the Beatles (i.e. locusts) but also implied that the power of the scorpion would prevail. (Charlie was a Scorpio.) In describing the locusts, Revelation said that "their faces were as the faces of men," yet "they had the hair of women," and wore "breastplates of fire," which Charlie interpreted as electric guitars. Another Revelation verse spoke of "fire and brimstone" coming from the four angels' mouths, which Charlie equated with the Beatles' music and lyrics.

Death Valley, by many, is seen as a place seemingly devoid of life. But contrary to popular opinion, life does indeed abound there, but it is only the heartiest and wiliest of animals that survive in this harsh environ, such as the coyote, whom -- if there ever was a Manson Family mascot -- it would be he; a creature alert and industrious, totally aware of itself and its surroundings, more scavenger than hunter, making use of the garbage and dead remains others have left behind -- in the same manner as Charlie and his pack became scavengers and dumpster divers.

Into this harsh, desert environment Charlie's Family came looking for some special sort of magic; to commune with nature and attain Coyotenoia. Manson's philosophy of Coyotenoia went as follows: "Christ on the cross, the coyote in the desert -- it's the same thing, man. The coyote is beautiful. He moves through the desert delicately, aware of everything, looking around. He hears every sound, smells every smell, sees everything that moves. He's always in a state of total paranoia and total paranoia is total awareness. You can learn from the coyote just like you learn from a child. A baby is born into the world in a state of fear. Total paranoia and awareness..."

Just like his coyote friends, Charlie's Family ran around in packs, constantly on guard against enemies. Coyotenoia took hold, as paranoia became a higher form of awareness. On the morning of the Barker Ranch raid, Charlie was camping out with a couple of the girls when a "big coyote came across the flat and up to me. He stopped just in front of me and was looking dead ahead with no fear. He kept it up for maybe half a minute, and a few times he kept looking back over in the direction he had come. And then I was looking out that way and I saw some rangers. They were coming across the desert floor. The big coyote was warning me!"

Under his "spell," Manson's camp followers snuffed out the lives of Sharon Tate and others during an evening of frenzied torture.

An aspect of the desert which fascinated Manson was that it was "a land where rivers ran upside down", a fact that appealed to Charlie's "no sense makes sense" worldview. Death Valley is an extension of the Great Basin, where literally thousands of streams run, although not one of them ever reaches the sea. Death Valley is the sink of the Amargosa River, most of which is below sea level. Here the stream beds are on top, and the water flows beneath the sand and gravel, a phenomenon that perplexed Charlie, who -- from the time he arrived in Death Valley -- began speaking of "a hole" in the desert that would lead his group to water, and perhaps even a lake and a place to live. Many days, Charlie would walk the desert floor in search of this mystical "hole." The idea of a "hole" was by no means a crazy one, since all water flowing into Death Valley eventually emerges elsewhere in the form of springs.

A parallel to Manson's vision of a magic hole was the Hopi legend of "Emergence from the Third World" which spoke of a large underground world from which the Hopi Nation would emerge -- back to the Earth's surface -- after Armageddon. Manson believed in the geological possibility of just such a hole. Evidently there have been claims in the past, as well, about a huge city-sized cavern beneath Death Valley, with a river running through it, fed by the mighty Amargosa.

One possible entrance to "The Hole" was thought to be the so-called Devil's Hole located in the northwest corner of Death Valley. The Devil's Hole, which is fenced off, is a forbidding pit of water, murky and ominous. In 1965, two young men went scuba diving at night into The Devil's Hole and were never seen again. Afterwards, rescue divers recovered only a flashlight, which suggested to many that The Devil's Hole led to a huge underground cavern.

On one occasion, Charlie sat crossed-legged before Devil's Hole for three straight days, meditating with all his metaphysical might, contemplating the ultimate meaning of this bottomless well. After the third day, it dawned on Charlie that the water in the Devil's Hole was the door -- or blocking mechanism -- preventing entrance into the Underworld. All Charlie had to do was find a way to suck the water out, and -- lo and behold! -- the secret passageway would be revealed!

You can drive up to the spot but its fenced off now courtsey of land management and a rare species of fish says Steve Groppe when asked how deep the hole is:
"I have no idea about the depth. The reason it is fenced in is because it is home to some ancient "pupfish:. They send divers down every so often to count them.
A google on "Pupfish" will give you the story." So much for Charles Manson and the Hole.
Photo copyright Steve Groppe. Courtsey www.CharlieManson.com

According to Bourke Lee's "Death Valley Men", in the 1930's two miners were working near Death Valley's Wingate Pass when they fell through the bottom of a mine shaft and into a immense cavern. The miners followed the cavern 20 miles north where they discovered an underground city housing the remains of mummies who wore armbands and held golden spears. Other artifacts included giant statues and gold bars, which seemed to confirm long whispered Paiute legends about an ancient, underground city located in the area.

During this same period, Dr. F. Bruce Russell claimed to have stumbled upon this same underground civilization, which included the discovery of eight-foot-tall mummies and American Indian artifacts.

Additionally, Dr. Russell discovered a multitude of other caves in the area, and spent the next fifteen years exploring them. In 1947, Russell raised funding for an expedition to excavate the caves; in response he received ridicule from his colleagues in the scientific community, and could find no one to accompany him in said expedition until he actually returned with the artifacts in question to prove they actually existed. Determined to succeed, Russell set off into the desert and was never heard from again.

Charles Manson was looking for an entrance to the inner earth.
A marker is posted near the spot where he thought an entrance existed and has been photographed by Steve Groppe.
The latest on Manson can be found at www.CharlieManson.com
Photo copyright Steve Groppe.

On the night of October 12th, 1969 a contingent of Inyo County sheriff's officers, National Park Rangers and California Highway patrol raided Barker Ranch just after dusk. When the cops burst into the Barker Ranch house, about a half dozen Manson Family members, sitting around a table, were ordered outside, lined up, and searched. Missing, however, was their most sought after prize, Manson himself.

One of the officers decided to recheck the ranch house, which was completely dark inside, except for a single candle burning. Taking the candle, the officer searched through the rooms and, on entering the bathroom, was forced to move the candle around to discern objects. As the officer lowered the candle toward the wash basin -- and noticed a small cupboard below it -- he saw long hair protruding from the partially open cupboard, an incredibly small space for a person to contort their body into. Without a word, a gnome-like figure emerged from the cupboard, unfolding himself, none other than Charlie Manson, who was subsequently apprehended and taken into custody for the Tate-LaBianca murders.

YOU CAN'T GO WRONG WITH GORIGHTLY!

A certified "crackpot historian" and 23rd degree Discordian, Adam Gorightly has been chronicling fringe culture in an illuminating manner for over two decades. An active contributor to the 'zine revolution of the late '80s and early '90s, Adam's byline was a familiar sight in many cutting-edge mags. His articles have appeared in numerous publications such as The Excluded Middle, UFO Magazine, Paranoia, SteamShovel Press, and FourTwoFour, the largest soccer magazine in Great Britain.

Adam has the following books to his credit: *The Shadow Over Santa Susana: Black Magic, Mind Control and the Manson Family Mythos; The Prankster and the Conspiracy: The Story of Kerry Thornley and How He Met Oswald and Inspired the Counterculture; Death Cults; The Beast of Adam Gorightly: Collected Rantings 1992-2004* and *James Shelby Downard's Mystical War.*

His older Podcasts are archived at http://gorightly.podomatic.com/
while the new stuff is located at "Transmissions From A Dying Planet"
http://gorightly.wordpress.com/

Death Valley : Breathtakingly Beautiful. Mysterious, and Deadly- Photo: Jon Sullivan

1:17

by Paul Dale Roberts, HPI Ghostwriter

Before I write the details of HPI's investigation at Bodie, I will give you the highlights of some of the legends, stories and descriptions of Bodie.

- A. ***The Curse of Bodie.*** If you take any items from Bodie, the resident ghosts that protect this ghost town will make sure you have misfortune. Many items taken from Bodie are shipped back to the Park Rangers, because of the curse.

- B. ***Lady of the Night.*** A woman with a long blue dress is sometimes sighted under a moonlight floating through the fields.

- C. Fights and murders were a common everyday occurrence at Bodie. Things were so bad, that when a young girl knew she was moving to Bodie with her parents, she wrote her grandmother the following message. "Goodbye God, I'm going to Bodie."

- D. The Reverend F.M. Warrington described Bodie as a Sea of Sin.

- E. When a little boy at Bodie didn't get a birthday cake, he set his kitchen table on fire. The fire spread throughout the town. When the fire was finally extinguished, 1/3 of the town had burned to the ground.

- F. One of the most haunted houses at Bodie is the Cain House. Jim Cain, a prominent businessman was caught having an affair with his Chinese maid. When the news got out, he committed suicide. When a Park Ranger's wife spent the night at the Cain House, she felt someone laying on top of her. She felt like she was being suffocated.

- G. Another haunted house in Bodie is the Mendocini House. Children are heard playing near the house and at times Park Rangers have heard the sound of a party, when there is no one in the house.

Now let's talk about the Scouting Mission/Investigation:

Dear lord, I don't know where to begin. Sierra Peterson - HPI Ghost hunter-in-Training/Scout and Bryan Coleman - ghost hunter/camera man spent the night with me at my home on Friday, July 25, 2008. We had to get up early Saturday for our Bodie Scouting Mission. You are probably wondering why I make mention of Bodie 1:17 in the title. . You will understand why after I finish this piece. Sierra Peterson brought her pit bull puppy named Bronte. Bronte will be on his first ghost hunting scouting mission and this officially makes him a ghost hunter-in-training. They say that animals have a sixth sense, so Bronte will be tested to see if he has these abilities in Bodie. Bryan, Sierra, Bronte and I hit the sack early, because 6 AM comes early. At 3:30 AM there is a knock at my door. Bryan wakes up startled and tells me that I have someone at my door. Who could be at my door at this ungodly hour? It was my drunk neighbor.

He was with some floozy girl and asking if I had anything to drink. Welcome to my neighborhood. Bryan and I, had a hard time getting back to sleep after this interruption. Luckily for Bronte and Sierra, they were sound asleep in the guest bedroom. 6 AM and the alarm goes off. How I wanted to go back to bed, but I knew I had to get up and prepare for this scouting mission. As I came out of the shower, I could hear two more ghost hunters-in-training at my door, it was LaShae 'Chiky' Tate and Veldena Ladson. Everyone was drinking their coffee down as quickly as possible, because it was time to hit the road and scramble over to Starbucks on Hwy 50 and Bradshaw to meet up with the other ghost hunter-in-training/scouts: Justin Schlesinger - formerly with P.I.B.A. (Paranormal Investigations Bay Area). Justin drove up from San Mateo, talk about dedication. We also had Laura Miller & Lynn Leino show up for this scouting mission. I gave everyone a briefing in regard to the requirements for this scouting mission and allowed Justin & Laura to discuss some of the history of Bodie, since both of them have been to Bodie before.

Bodie is quite a distance and not too many people want to take this long trek up to Bodie, especially with the cost of gas. But, if you do trek up to Bodie, make sure to stop at Silverfork Grill, 13196 Hwy 50, Kyburz, CA. You will be served by Tim Evoniuk, Josh Evoniuk and Brooke Meyer. They are the owners and are very hospitable. I had a ham and egg sandwich, served quickly and it was tremendously good. It really hit the spot for a hungry ghost writer/ghost hunter. As we left the Silverfork Grill, one of the passenger's stomach became upset and our four car caravan had to do an emergency pit stop, as our associate got sick in my car. This must be an omen about going to Bodie, but after my car was cleaned out, we kept on rolling towards Bodie. When you take long road trips, the appetite increases I have noticed. It was time to stop over at Pop's Galley Seafood, 241 Main Street, Bridgeport, CA. This place did not satisfy our appetites and I found myself longing for the Silverfork Grill. After I finished my lunch, I headed over to the very haunted Bridgeport Inn (see www.thebridgeportinn.com). I interviewed an employee of the Bridgeport Inn named Dennis Williams. He told me some scary ghost tales of this inn. How there was a guest that was told by a guy in a smoking jacket that he could go ahead and use the bathroom before him. The only thing is, there were no other guests on the floor. The guy in the smoking jacket was a ghost! Another guest named Jeannie, had a ghost call her by her name and that really scared her. Some guests have seen full body apparitions and it's common for glasses to sometimes jump off the shelves.

We finally reached Bodie. Bodie once was a thriving town that boasted 10,000 citizens. A town that attracted people because of the vein gold that was discovered. Towns like Dogtown, Monoville, Aurora and of course Bodie were places where people could make a fast fortune mining gold. The town is filled with history, such as how some men were found sinking a shaft at the Jupiter Mine in Bodie. The men were chased out of town, but later returned. A gunfight ensued. In the wake, a Bodie mine crew chief was killed and George Daly, the Jupiter Mine Superintendent was arrested and jailed in Bodie. There was talk of a lynching, George had to be transferred to Bridgeport for his own safety. There were robberies, like in 1884 when Tex Wilson robbed the Bodie & Lundy Stage and kidnapped a Chinese woman. Wilson was a leader of a gang that terrorized the citizens of Bodie on a constant basis, when he was finally jailed, there was talk of giving him a necktie party. Somehow he managed to escape the noose.

As for ghost stories, tourists have heard children playing and when they investigated where the laughter was originating from, they found no children. A rocking chair in one of the abandoned homes rocks on its own accord. There have been sightings of full body apparitions. There is a ghost of a little girl named Emily that is seen near the Bodie cemetery. Bryan Coleman was able to locate the gravesite. When we went to the Bodie cemetery we ran into Cathy Nease, Christina & Mike Pritchett, Jennifer Chamberlain & Rick Avery. Cathy tells us that she heard that HPI was coming up to Bodie to investigate and she brought her whole family to meet and greet us. It was an honor to meet this wonderful family that has an interest in the paranormal and historical places like Bodie. Bryan and I, interviewed many of the tourists and found out that many tourists that come to Bodie like Carol L. Rauch and a family from Austria, do believe in the paranormal and have experienced the paranormal for themselves.

An email I received from Christopher Shangley says: "When I went to Bodie during the Summer of 1987, I will never forget how I was watching this cowboy, who I thought was an actor walking around the fields. As I kept watching him he went into one of the buildings and walked right through a door! I knew then, that I saw a ghost! I told my wife and she just laughed at me!"

Bodie is a ghost town with a lot of history. It is a town that harbored violence, tragedy, illness and sudden deaths from the extreme weather conditions. I do believe this town has accumulated a lot of residual haunting activity. Perhaps also there is intelligent haunting activity here too. Probably the lost souls of residents that don't want to leave their beloved town. This Saturday, July 27, 2008, my scouts were equipped with digital audio recorders, video camera, digital cameras, EMF reader and walkie-talkies and they scouted every inch of Bodie. There was a lot of wind interference and perhaps too many tourists to actually pick up any solid EVPs. We hope after fully analyzing everything we collected, that we can prove that Bodie is a truly haunted ghost town. So far, my photographs show some orb activity, but we need EVP proof that there is really paranormal activity taking place in this ghost town.

The reason that I refer to Bodie 1:17 in the title is because we did not want to go back at night the same way we came in during the day. The trip to Bodie was treacherous, driving around curvy cliffs with no guard rails. We took the main freeways back, such as the 395 through Reno and finally reaching 80 back to Sacramento. I rather take a longer route and be safe than sorry. We finally all arrived home at 1:17 AM. What a long day it was. Getting up at 6 AM starting out at 8 AM and not getting home until 1:17 AM. Thanks goes to the fine Nevada police officer that pulled over when Bryan and I pulled over on the side of the road and gave us directions to get back to Sacramento. He looked at me and saw the desperation in my face, as I said..."officer we are lost, we're just trying to get back to Sacramento!" Nevada's finest were ready and willing to assist lost weary ghost hunters!

Bodie is a very unique ghost town. I really wish we could have the town to ourselves to do a proper and through investigation. If anything, we received a historical aspect of this town. A town that had business and professional men, mine-operators, miners, saloon-keepers, hundreds of gamblers, hundreds of prostitutes, many Chinese, a considerable number of Mexicans, and a quantity of bad men. Desperadoes that came to visit Bodie from all parts of the United States. They lived under the code of cheating and gambling, gun-fighting, stage robbing and other criminal acts. The Bad Men from Bodie was a commonly used phrase when describing Bodie. Bodie was more known for its lawlessness than for its riches.

Before I end this article, I want to let everyone know, if you want some stones or gems for blessing of your home, a place you may want to check out is: www.larzodesign.com Ask for Larz 'Red' Lapin, she is very knowledgeable in regard to stone or gems that give off positive energy for a home.

As for Bronte, the pit bull – ghost hunter-in-training. Well, Bronte was pretty pooped out from this trip and didn't find any ghosts for us. Maybe next time.

Paul Dale Roberts, HPI Paranormal Investigative Reporter, Ghost hunter
Haunted and Paranormal Investigations International
www.HPI.paranormal.net
WPRT Paranormal Radio - Content Editor
Email: JazmaPika@cs.com

Paranormal Cellular Hotline: 916 203 7503 (for comments on this story).
If you have a possible investigation call: 1-888-709-4HPI
Copyright © 2008 Paul Dale Roberts, HPI Ghostwriter Copyright © 2008 all rights reserved.

Death Valley Known for the 20 mule team borax freight system

From the Sea To the Sand
Lost Ships of the Desert
by Harold O. Weight

One of the greatest writers the West has ever known!

There are those who will tell you the Lost Ship is only the triangular bulk of old Signal Mountain (above) distorted by heat waves in top the broken hulk and shattered spars of a phantom Spanish galleon. But the oldtimers swear that somewhere in the ancient sea-bed of the Salton Sink (shown below near the base of the Santa Rosas) the wreck of a centuries-old vessel lies buried . .

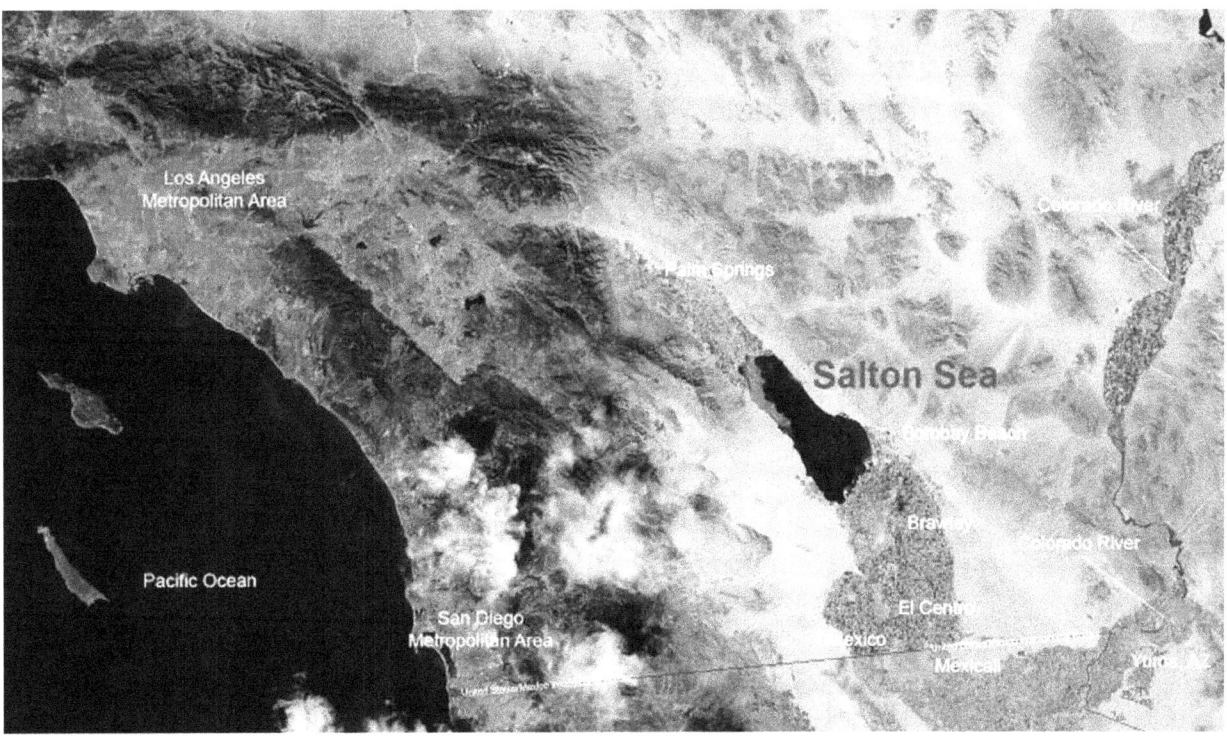

Spot on map where it is believed the lost ship might be located.

LOST SHIP OF THE DESERT

Somewhere in the great Salton Basin, or the Laguna Salada or the delta of the Colorado River, lie the bones of an ancient ship stranded hundreds of years ago — seen now and again by desert wanderers or by Indians. That is one of the most persistent legends of the far Southwest — and there is every reason to believe that such a ship does or could exist.

That is not to say that the ship — be it Viking, or Spanish, or Chinese, or Russian, or even from Mu — sailed into what is now desert when the great California Gulf was open all the way to he slopes of San Gorgonio Pass. Neither does it follow, necessarily, that scientific doctrine is right, and that the Gulf and the Basin have not been joined by navigable water for numberless thousands of years.

During the centuries since man has been navigating the oceans of the world, the course of the mighty Colorado River has changed countless times. The great sink, whose lower levels are now occupied by the Salton Sea, forty-odd miles long and up to 12 miles wide, probably was filled and evaporated away and was refilled many and many a time. A huge fresh-water lake — called both Lake Cahuilla and Blake Sea — is believed to have occupied a great part of the sink, including present El Centro and many towns and rich farms of the Imperial Valley, the lower portions of Coachella Valley, and other parts of the Colorado Desert. The larger this lake, the narrower the barrier would have been between it and the head of tide water in the Gulf — and the greater the possibility that a ship, carried on some great equinoctial tide and meeting Colorado flood waters, might have been shunted into the lake.

There is no question that even in the early years of this century, a fairly large ship could have navigated the channel of Hardy's Colorado, at high tide, to the point where the tide and river current battled, then have gone with the river into Laguna Salada. As for the delta — many ships might have been carried well into its flats by the great tidal bore which, in the spring, sluices up the channels at the head of the Gulf. Difference between high and low tide in this area has been recorded at more than 37 feet, and rises of up to 50 feet have been reported. During the days when there was heavy shipping on the Colorado, this rise and fall was used to dry-dock ships in a tidal basin at Puerta Isabel, once a shipyard.

With these conditions, why doubt that more than one ship was trapped in some areas of this strange old-sea-bed world? Starting in the middle 1500s, Spanish adventurers, explorers, missionaries, pearlers and smugglers dared the exceedingly frequent dreadful storms and the violent tides of the great Gulf. There was also a time when English and Dutch pirates harried the shipping even within the Gulf. Many ships disappeared. Some were destroyed by storms, driven hundreds of miles off their courses, beached and sunk. Some were captured by the pirates. The crews of some fell victims to savage natives when they landed. Mutinous crews sailed others away. Between the years of 1712 and 1717, the Jesuits alone lost a ship a year to storms. In the autumn of 1717, a tremendous three-day hurricane accompanied by continuous rain swept the peninsula of Lower California, destroying much of the work of the Jesuits. During it, two small pearling ships disappeared from La Paz and were never seen again.

The Lost Ship of the Desert might have been one of these. It might have been one of the ships of the pearl smugglers, who operated secretly after Viceroy Enriquez, about 1702, prohibited pearl fishing without a special license from him. The next year, a terrible storm destroyed one smuggler ship, while the other two of the fleet which had been pearling among the islands of the Gulf, were beached at Loreto. If might even have been one of the pirate ships. According to the chronicles of Hakluyt, the Content, one of Thomas Cavendish's ships, loaded with gold and silver and silks and perfumes from captured Spanish galleons, was last seen by her companion ships in the mouth of the Gulf near Cape San Lucas. The other ship reach England safely. The Content was never heard from again, and Philip A. Bailey, who has a section on the Lost Ship in his book Golden Mirages, speculates that her captain might have thought that the Gulf was the long sought Straights of Anian, and attempted a short cut to the Atlantic.

But our choice for the Lost Ship — if it be a Spanish one — goes back before that. In his account of the conquest of Mexico, Captain Bernal Diaz del Castillo, bold companion of Cortez, relates: "In the month of May, 1532, the Marquis del Valle (Cortez) sent two ships from the port of Acapulco, to make discoveries in the South Seas. They were commanded by a captain named Diego Hurtado de Mendoza, who, without going far to sea, or doing anything worthy of relating, had the misfortune of a mutiny among the troops, in consequence whereof, one ship, of which the mutineers took possession, returned to New Spain to the great disappointment of Cortez. As for Hurtado, neither he nor his vessel were ever more heard of."

If mutineers took over Mendoza's ship, the Iqueque, the Gulf would have been a logical hiding place for them. It was the spot that the mutineer Jiminez head for, a short time later, when he took over a ship which Cortez sent out to search for Mendoza. Jiminez was the first known to have discovered and landed on the peninsula of Lower California, and he and his companions were killed by the natives there. The expedition of Francisco de Ulloa, which went to the head of the Gulf, was also searching for Mendoza, as well as exploring.

Harold O. Weight might have suspected that this friendly mule driver might have come across a lost ship but never spoken about it.

But there would seem to be an even stronger possibility that the ancient ship which has been seen by at least some desert people arrived five centuries before Cortez. Does it sound impossible that a Viking ship sailed our western coasts a thousand years ago? It seems even more impossible that Indians who had never seen the Vikings could have imagined a correct description for one of their ships. And it is possible that one or more of their ships could have traveled the true Northwest Passage, above Canada and Alaska, in a warmer epoch. That voyage has been made in modern times. And the Norsemen were colonizing Greenland and adventuring on to the shores of North America around the year 1000. A colony existed on the west coast of Greenland for hundreds of years — a Norse searching party being sent to discover what happened to it and rescue survivors in 1354. A sword, ax head and shield grip dating to about 1000 and declared authentic Norse work were found in western Ontario province, Canada.

Dane and Mary Coolidge, in their book The Last of the Seris, make the definite statement that blue-eyed, yellow haired Vikings did come to Tiburon Island in the Gulf long ago, and that members of the expedition became the founders of the blue-eyed fair-complexioned Mayo Indians on the Mayo River, Sonora. The Seri Indians of Tiburon have legends and songs of these early white giants, who came in a long boat driven by sweeps, who were whalers living in big houses by the sea, in their own land. Whose weapons were the bow and arrow and spear. With them, said the Seris, was a red-haired woman, wife of the captain, who wore her in big braids down her back and was even fairer than the men, who dressed in heavy clothes and had a big cloak or mantle. (Freydis, daughter of Eric the Red, was in command of a Viking ship to the east coast of North America, in 1014, so Viking women did sail.)

The blonde strangers stayed on Tiburon Island a year and four months, and then they sailed away with four families of Seri, promising to bring them back when they returned. But they never did return to Tiburon. Perhaps their long boat was grounded and abandoned somewhere in the Salton Sink and they walked out — either to Arizona where there was an early legend of blonde and redheaded Indians — or even as far as the Mayo River.

Probably there are ships of a later date in the desert. When the excitement about reported discovery of the Lost Ship was high in 1870, a Los Angeles newspaper explained that the ship undoubtedly was a 23-foot sloop, built in Los Angeles in 1862, for use on the Colorado River. Attempts had been made, for some reason, to transport the boat overland, and it had been abandoned in the desert when the mule-power broke down. Part of this account was a tongue-in-cheek yarn by Major Horace Bell. Bell in his Reminiscences of a Ranger stated that the ship had been discovered by the great explorer Joshua Talbot. Talbot, was an editor of the San Bernardino Guardian, and he did go on an expedition to locate the ship, but did not see it and soon had enough of the quest.

But by the time a San Diego publication had garbled the story, Talbot became the original gold seeker who attempted to haul the boat across to the Colorado near La Paz. In this form, the yarn — becoming as fabulous as the Lost Ship legend could possibly be — has furnished much grist for the writers of "debunking" magazine articles. In the most recent one, the little sloop has grown to a scow 60 feet in length, drawn by oxen.

There are other ships and boats which have been lost — and in the case of Lieut. Ives' steamer Explorer, which he used in exploring the Colorado River in 1858, found. The nearly buried hull of the Explorer was found on the delta in 1928.

But these are not the Lost Ship. It was a legend and being sought at the time the little sloop was being build in Los Angeles; its description did not fit Ives' boat.

Following are a few of the stories and legends which surround the Lost Ship.

**Copyright 1953, by the Calico Press,
Twentynine Palms, California**

Somewhere out in the Mojave a lost ship may be lurking.
Harold O. Weight wrote some of the most incredible stories
revolving around desert life and legends.
He was also an amazing photographer
as this picture will attest.

The weird Yuha Badlands in Imperial County, all once part of the Gulf of California. Signal Mountain, (in background left), marks the Mexican border. To the right and beyond it is the basin of Laguna Salada in Baja California. Some oldtimers believed that the lost ship was only a mirage of Signal Mountain itself, caused by the distorting heat waves of the terrible midsummer temperature. Photo by Harold Weight.

A Ghost of the Vikings?
by Paul Wilhelm

The desert is the haunt of mystery. Sometimes men hear whispers of its past. They go seeking beyond the shimmering mirage. Into the silence they plod. A few are lost. A few return from uncharted desolation bringing back strange tales. An Indian tribe that has never seen a white man. A mine with a door of iron. Or a lost ship half buried in the sandy bed of an old sea.

The tales of the lost ships of the Colorado Desert have gathered moss, they have been told so many times. Although logical explanation gives credence to a few tales, they've been more or less exploded. Yet the fascination persists. Here's why:

In the bottom of every old seabed throughout he world bones of adventurous men on argosies to unknown lands have been found sealed with the ooze of stratified muds; it would be strange then if this particular ancient sea bed in the Colorado Desert of California was the exception. True, it is eons since a genuine sea flooded this valley, yet men have sailed in ships longer than our knowledge of history penetrates.

So there seems nothing impossible in the stories one hears. There's the tale of a ship with hexagonal spars, its wreck found by Indians all but covered with sand far up the meanderings of a dry wash in the Chocolate Mountains. One story, published years ago in their magazine supplement of the Los Angeles Examiner, told of a Spanish galleon loaded with a king's ransom in precious stones, its wreck sighted in sand dunes northwest of Indio. One old desert vagabond who visited my oasis at Thousand Palms years back told me he had once found parts of a Chinese junk sand-and-clay buried near the oyster beds at Willis Palms.

And so the many stories are told and retold. They may all be true. For there probably were many ships. Wrecks of ships have come to light in the remotest parts of the earth.

But the story that seems most authentic is the one of the old Viking ship in the Colorado Desert. I've heard it a score of times and each time it seems more plausible. Here are the facts:

Down from the little mining town of Julian in the San Diego hinterland some years ago rode Mr. and Mrs. Louis Botts. That night they camped at Agua Caliente springs. In their first evening at the springs they had a visitor, a prospector who swapped them yarn for yarn — but all his stories centered on gold...

Until he drew from his wallet a few faded photographs of a "wreck of a ship of some kind" which he had found exploring for gold in the rough country down by the Mexican border.

Myrtle Botts, who is the librarian at Julian, studied the small worn prints. Then she exclaimed, "Why this is the skeleton of a very ancient ship! It's the type used in the period when Eric the Red made his voyages to America. Look, "she said, pointing to the picture of a ship half buried beside a rocky bank, "there's the high serpent bow, the curved ribs — an ancient long boat!"

But their visitor remained indifferent to the questions plied on him; his mind was intent on gold. "Can't see what's so strange about finding a boat in this desert. There used to be water here."

When Mrs. Botts asked, "Why did you take the photographs?" the prospector replied, "Seemed sorta funny finding a boat so far from water." He was a matter-of-fact fellow and had imagination only for gold. "Boats just ain't in my line," he said as he tired of the questioning and eased off toward his camp.

In the morning the prospector had drifted on; the Botts never saw him again. Upon returning to Julian, Mrs. Botts thumbed through every book on early explorations. There was little to find of Norsemen voyaging towards "lands west." Nor did yearly searches that the Botts made uncover the ancient wreck.

But Myrtle Botts is positive the old serpent-prowed ship exists. And though the dust of centuries covers the hopes of dead voyagers on adventuresome argosies to unknown lands, she is certain that one day that lost ship of a vanished sea will be found!

From "Paul Wilhelm's Desert Column,
" The Indio Date Palm, Indio, California, October 4, 1951.

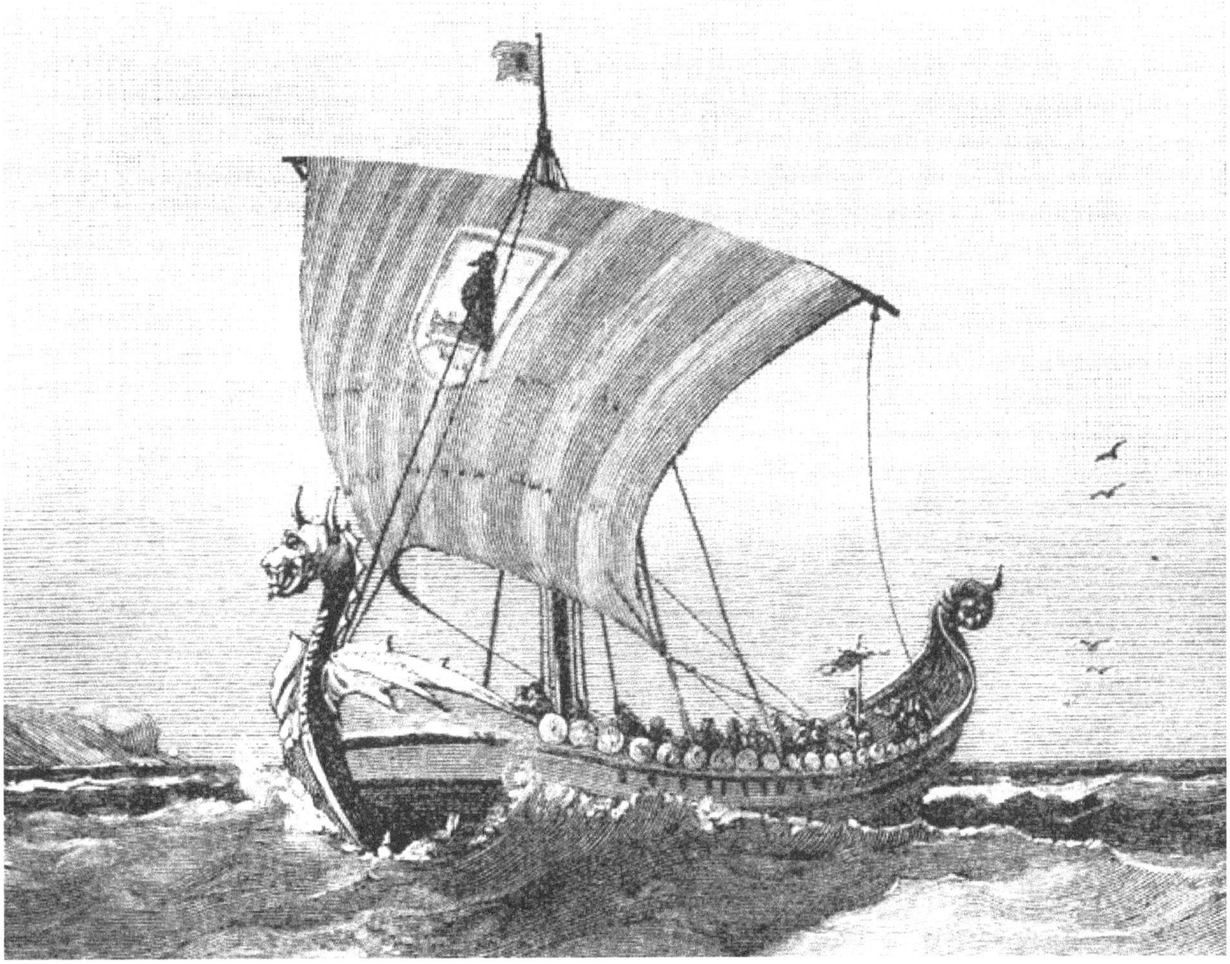

Mullett Island, Salton Sea, Cal. Davis

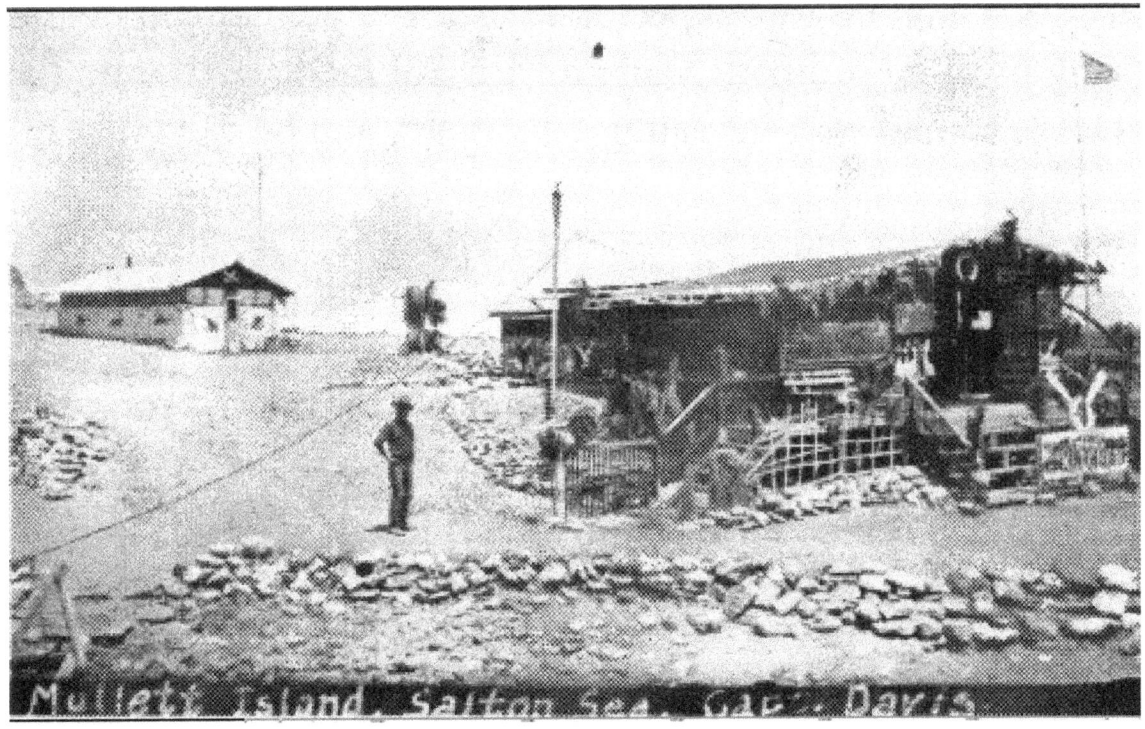

Mysteries and Haunts of the Mojave Desert - Secrets of Death Valley

Artist's Rendition of a Spanish Galleon in the Desert
From the internet, no source given, no artist or copyright information

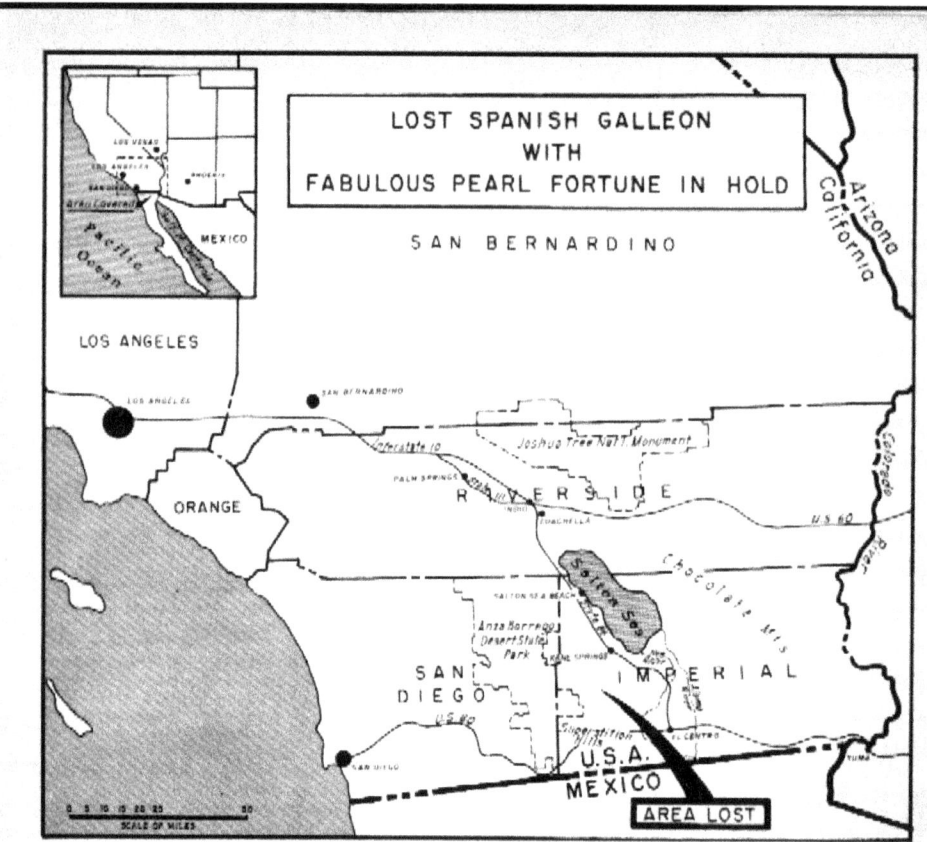

Mystery of the Desert
by J. A. Guthrie

"What is the greatest unsolved mystery of the Southwest desert?" asked W.W. McCoy?

"It is whether 300 years ago three ships sailed up the Colorado River and into the Salton Sea," the old man of the Yuma Trail answered his own question.

"My old friend Herman Ehrenberg, of the Colorado River, found in Arizona an Indian tribe, members of which had blue eyes and red hair. He spent his life seeking to solve that mystery, for the Indians of red hair were born long before white men reached that region.

"Ehrenberg took me to the Salton Sea and there we talked to Big Chief Cabazon. I was interpreter, and Cabazon told us of the history of his tribe as it was handed down to him by chiefs before him. To be a big chief, a man must be able to tell his tribe the stories of many big chiefs before him. These recitals may take days.

"Cabazon told us that as near as he could judge three hundred years before, two ships had sailed into the Salton Sea. The men had landed and taken timber out of the mountains. That was the story handed down to him.

"Ehrenberg spent many years investigating that story, and it was his conclusion that three ships loaded with exiles from some country in Europe — he knew all the historic facts about the sailing of the ships — had reached the Pacific and sailed up the Colorado. He believed that one of the ships had been captured by a tribe on the Arizona side and that the men had been killed and the women carried into captivity."

In the late sixties there were stories, even printed in the frontier newspapers, of the sighting of an ancient ship in the hills in the Salton Sea region, and expeditions were organized. The story vanished with the explanation it was a mirage and there are among the old desert travelers still alive men who actually saw the mirage of the desert ship.

Salton Sea Sink in the 1800's before the Colorado River
flooded the sink turning it back to a sea.

"I have seen wonderful mirages from the Salton Sea Sink," said McCoy. "From one spot on the same day I saw in the early days, the city of Tucson; an emigrant party on the Gila River, and so complete was the detail that I could see the whip on the arm of the driver; and when that faded away I saw Fort Yuma and last the harbor of San Diego."

Whether the story of Big Chief Cabazon had in actual fact been based on a mirage seen by the Indians as the Spaniards were exploring the coast of the Pacific or whether the ships of ancient times actually sailed into the desert sink which in the centuries past has receded and risen again, the oldtimers on the Yuma Trail say will never be known.

From an interview with W.W. McCoy in the Los Angeles Examiner, June 15, 1919

Salton Sea Sink today following massive federal government
intervention to restore the sea to its natural state after industry
had polluted the sea making it a toxic waste dump.

The Lost Spanish Galleon
by L. Burr Belden

O.J. Fisk, prominent San Bernardino pioneer, who in his younger years prospected and mined over much of the Southwest, believes he has a solution to the century old legend of a Spanish ship said buried under the bottom of the Salton Sea. An account of an early Spanish voyage, coupled with the testimony of a Cahuilla Indian and a Harquehala, Arizona, prospector has satisfied Fisk that a Spaniard sailed into what is now the Salton Sea centuries ago and walked away from his marooned craft. But for the fact that the Salton Sink of 50 years ago is now the Salton Sea, Fisk is confident he could locate the remains of the old ship without too much trouble.

In 1892, Jim Fisk was mining in the Julian-Banner district of San Diego County and doing some prospecting as well. He became acquainted with a Cahuilla Indian, an elderly man who had once lived in the almost forgotten village of Old Santa Rosa on the Imperial Valley side of the mountains.

The Indian, whose name is recalled by Fisk as Harra Chee, told Fisk about the location of some gold north of Banner. Fisk was interested, bought some grub, and the two set out. The Indian took him along the east face of the mountains until the two were about west of the present Borrego settlement.

There the Indian showed Fisk a hole. He found a show of color, but not enough gold to pay working. Following a day's digging, Fisk and the Indian cooked their meal and then watched the shadows fall on the desert below.

Then the Indian told him a story. His grandfather had seen white men first come to this desert in a white bird. The white bird stayed a long time down there. The bird's wings fell down and the sand covered it up.

This story of the lost ship and the map (left) appeared in the San Bernadino Sun-Telegram, February 15, 1953, and are reproduced through permission of L. Burr Belden.

The young prospector returned to Julian the next day and thought little of the Indian's story until some years later over in Arizona he heard a prospector from the Vicksburg or Harequehala district tell of having stumbled on the remains of what appeared to be a Spanish ship in the Salton Sink, the shifting sand having uncovered part of it.

Fisk pressed the miner for more details, found the location would have been almost east of Kane Springs at the south end of the sink. The two planned to meet later and find the old ship but the Colorado River turned the Salton Sink into the Salton Sea and ended all such plans.

Even Gene Autry had to deal with The Lost Desert Ship

Now retired, Fisk has devoted much of his time to historical study. He learned that the tribe to which his guide of 1892 belonged had no word for ancestor more remote than grandfather and that the "grandfather" Harra Chee told of might well have been a remote ancestor, whose tale of the white man arriving in the big bird on the water was passed down from generation to generation.

Early Spanish writings have indicated a minor Colorado Desert flood early in the 16th century, a flood that abated before making any lake of great dimensions such as the present Salton Sea.

What Fisk believes clinches his theory is the account that in the early 17th century, when Spanish maps showed California as an island, five ships ascended the Gulf of California on a pearl fishing expedition. The ships became separated in a storm, and only four returned.

The fifth ship was captained by one Juan Iturbe who showed up later at Acapulco without his vessel but with a strange tale of having found a narrow passage north which ended in a lake around which he sailed several times, only to find the entry passage gone and no way out.

Fisk believes Iturbe's ship was the Indian's white bird and the same ship, buried in the sand noted by the Arizona prospector.

The Quest For The Lost Ship
by the San Bernadino Guardian, September 10, 1870

(Taken from the Los Angeles News)

INTERESTING DISCOVERY: By many it has been held as a theory that the Yuma Desert was once an ocean bed. At intervals, pools of salt water have stood for a while in the midst of the surrounding waste of sand, disappearing only to rise again in the same or other localities. A short time since, one of these saline lakes disappeared and a party of Indians reported the discovery of a 'big ship' left by the receding waters. A party of Americans at once proceeded to the spot and found embedded in the sands the wreck of a large vessel. Nearly one-third of the forward part of the ship, or barque, is plainly visible. The stump of the bowsprit remains and portions of the timbers of teak are perfect. The wreck is located 40 miles north of the San Bernardino and Fort Yuma Road and 30 miles west of Dos Palmas, a well-known watering place on the desert . . .

San Bernadino Guardian, December 31, 1870:

THE SEARCH FOR THE LOST SHIP: For years there have been rumors of a ship being found upon the desert from 40 to 50 miles in a southwest direction from Dos Palmos station, between San Bernadino and La Paz, and a few weeks ago Mssrs. Clusker, Caldwell and Johnson started from San Bernadino to verify the fact. Passing south of Martinez toward the Lake they found themselves in a morass and that it was impossible to proceed farther . . . Charley Clusker organized another party of himself and Mssrs. Hubble, Ferster and West, and with a four horse team came to Martinez and deflecting farther to the south crossed to within a short distance of the old Ft. Yuma road, but owing to the absence of fresh water, were compelled to return — not however until Clusker became convinced that he saw the ship far out in the lake . . .

The indefatigable Charley rested a day or two in San Bernadino and organized another expedition composed of J.A. Talbott, one of the editors of this paper, D.S. Ferster and F.J. West. We had water capacity for 108 gallons, provisions for two months and four good horses and wagon . . . We came his time by a difficult route — that of the old Ft.

Yuma road via Warner's Ranch and Cariso Creek station . . . here filling up our casks with water we boldly plunged out into the desert, intending to go as far as our water would permit and sending the wagon back for a fresh supply if we failed to find it . . . Charley was determined to thoroughly prospect as he went. After about 20 days my business required my return, and taking two of the horses, with Ferster we crossed the intervening space between the Laguna and Martinez station, a distance of about 60 miles. The next day Ferster returned to the wagon, and we came home on one of Gus Knight's wagons, glad to see San Bernadino once more. We left the boys in good spirits, confident they will yet find the ship, but as for ourselves, as we have not lost any ships, we do not feel inclined to undertake another expedition to find one.

***

San Bernadino Guardian, January 14, 1871:

RETURN OF THE SHIP PROSPECTORS. On Tuesday evening last, Charley Clusker and party returned to town, we are sorry to say, unsuccessful. . . .

Strange Salton Sea, below sea level in the great Salton Sink - Salton Sea in background, with San Andreas Fault in foreground

The Serpent-Necked "Canoa"
by Ed Stevens

In 1917, an old Indian rode into the yard of our ranch in Imperial Valley. He was looking for work, he said, He had come into the Valley to pick cotton, but his eyes bothered him and he could not see well enough to pick. He came from the Juarez Mountains of Lower California and gave the name of Jesús Almanerez. I think he was a Santa Rosa Indian.

I told him that I had a lot of mesquite wood to chop, and that suited him. But he refused to stay in the bunkhouse up by the ranch. He went down to the Alamo River and built an arrowed remade.

He was a very quiet and polite old man, with never much to say. He was with me three years and was always reliable.

When the first Christmas came, we had a big dinner. Then I loaded up a big platter with food and took it down to old Jesús' camp. He was greatly pleased that we would remember him on Christmas Day. So after filling up with all the food he could hold, he became rather talkative. I asked him what he had worked at in his younger days. He said he had worked in the timber and mines and as a woodchopper. Then I asked him if he had ever found any gold or treasure of any kind.

This is the story he told me:

"I was chopping wood with a crew of wood choppers just off the Laguna Salada. We were packing it on mule back up to the end of the sand hills where a wagon loaded it and hauled it to the Yuha Oil Well, which was then being drilled. (Ed. Note: In the Yuha Badlands, a few miles southeast of Coyote Wells, and south of U.S. Highway 80.) I think about 1898.

"It was late summer and the west winds were beginning to blow. For twelve days it blew, and then followed a big rain. We were about out of provisions so I loaded up a ten-mule train of wood and started out. The trail led along the foothills. I soon found the going too slippery for the loaded mules. So I turned off into the sand hills, which were wet and easier going.

"I had only gone a few miles when my lead mule stopped and pointed his ears. Looking that way I saw half buried in the side of a big sand hill a large canoa. (He meant a large canoe or ship. E.S.) It had a long neck and the head of a beast, and copper plates along the sides."

Since his boyhood spent with the Santa Ysabel Indians, Ed Stevens has been a life-long friend of the Indian people of the Imperial Valley and the San Diego mountains. From them he has learned many stories not usually told except among themselves.

"I got out of there as fast as my mules could travel. I unloaded the wood, got our provisions, and went back along the foothill trail. When I got back to camp, I drew my pay and left for the mountains, never to go back there again.

He told me that seeing tat canoa was a bad sign, and to save himself he had to leave immediately. I believe there must have been some legend about that ship among the Indians down there. Probably others had seen it, and unable to explain its strange appearance had regarded it as a "bad sign."

I was busy farming at the time, and did not have the time to pay much attention to the story. But it continued to bother me, and a few years later, I went to the Irrigation District office and asked for an old map of the area in Old Mexico. They gave me one of a survey of 1910.

As soon as I looked it over, I could see that it would have been very easy, even then, for a boat to get into the Laguna Salada in late spring when the Colorado would be in flood and meeting a high tide. The tide water went almost to Volcanic Lake. A boat could have come up the channel on the tide until it met the river current, then turned back and followed the river to Laguna Salada, where it became stranded as the flood receded.

I traced out and followed the old wagon road from the Yuha well drill hole to the head of the Laguna Salada in 1930, and I believe traces of that road would be visible yet. But I never had time to search the sand hills for a ship.

[image: area map] From this 1910 survey of the Irrigation District of the Imperial Valley, it is easy to see how a ship could have gone up Hardy's Colorado, from the Gulf, then been deflected into Laguna Salada.

Viking Ship.. Snake Necked Canoe

Above Viking Ship on Display in Ireland

Butcherknife Ike and the Lost Ship
by Adelaide Arnold

When she was a girl at Morningside Ranch, near Hemet, Adelaide Arnold came to know many of the desert prospectors. Butcherknife Ike was one of the strangest. Adelaide, noted writer, is just completing her new book, "Traveler's Moon," sequel to "Son of the First People."

From before World War One into the early Twenties, Butcherknife Ike often stopped at our ranch, Morningside, when starting on or coming from prospecting expeditions in the southern desert. Morningside lay near the mouth of San Juan Bautista Canyon, southeast of Hemet, and the canyon eventually led up to Coahuila. From there the prospectors crossed over to Coyote Canyon and went down into the Borrego Desert.

Butcherknife Ike - I do not know how he came by the name - was very irregular in his appearances and he very rarely had any greeting when he arrived. He just appeared in the drive, with his burros tagging after him. He would take their leads off and they would immediately begin to get their meal off the lawn - and also off some of Mother's roses. He would camp down in the eucalyptus grove.

Generally we had tea, late afternoons about five, on the lawn by the house. And if he was camped below, Butcherknife Ike would wander in and join us. Mother would get out a big cup and fill it with tea, hot and strong, the way he liked it. She would give him the cup and he would hold it and she would put one lump of sugar in. The cup was still stationary, so she would put in another lump. Finally there would be five or six lumps, and then he would take it over to the little flume which ran across the lawn, and sit down and hunch himself along until he could feel the flume against his back. There he would sit, perfectly silent, drinking his tea. He'd gulp down the tea and come back and have another cup - sometimes four or five cups.

In between cups, he'd sit and think a little, and then he'd put the cup up against his face - almost make a suction cup of it - and a long, sucking sound came as he got out the sugar in the bottom. When his cup was returned, it was just as clean as a whistle, though he never used a spoon.

I remember, mostly, the way he gestured with his long hands when he talked, and his faded blonde hair and the way it had a ripple down it and was quite long, falling on his neck. Of course he started on his trips with it clipped - almost what now we would call a crew cut. But when he appeared in summer, it was a page bob, almost. His eyes were very, very blue.

He was a strange man. He never talked to the other prospectors if they were there, and they said he always went out alone. When he first came, he rarely looked at us. He always looked at something on the horizon when he talked. If he talked. And he always looked at you sideways when you asked where he was going. He was so secretive always. If there was another prospector around you couldn't drag out of him the exact place he was going.

The day that he told us about the ship, Father had asked him where he had been. For Father occasionally he would give some details. But as always, it was quite disconnected. All his talk was that way. He'd remove you suddenly to Death Valley, or into Arizona. Just jerk out a few adventures - and then he didn't want to talk about it if you began to pin him down about the exact locations.

And he had apparently been thinking of the strangeness of this adventure. I fancy he wouldn't have talked to us at all, if it hadn't been on his mind.

He had been down by Laguna Salada, in Baja California, he said. He was returning from Laguna Salada. And he was going through by Split Mountain Canyon to look for some mineral he thought he had seen there before. It was about the Fourth of July, I believe - and hot. And he came in the dark to a place where there was a big sand dune. In telling it, he said over and over again, that it was no place for a big sand due to be. It was flat there. The arroyo was flat.

There was a bad wind blowing and he went over and took shelter in the lee of the big dune. On that big dune he discovered there was a sort of shelf of sand, below the highest point. That seemed to be the best place to camp, so he climbed up. There wasn't much around there to make a fire, but he made one of quail brush. He explained that, so we would know how little the fire was and how quickly it would have burned out. He cooked his beans and made his coffee.

Sometime in the night he waked. There, where he had made his little fire, he saw a tongue of flame coming up through the sand. He had an expression he used when he was talking about anything unusual. He would drop his voice and say: "I was kinda curious."

He was kind of curious about that flame where no flame should be. So he lighted his lantern and brought it over and he scooped and dug down through the sand. And presently - about two feet down, he said - he came to a heavy piece of wood. By the light of his lantern, he could see that it was worked wood.

In the morning, he dug some more, and he uncovered the beam and under it was another curved beam, attached to it. And on the beam underneath were barnacles. Old barnacles that crumbled.

"I scrabbled around a little bit," he went on, "and I saw it was a ship. I walked down the dune and I saw where the sand had covered it. It was a big ship. An old ship from the Gulf."

"Did you tell anyone about it?" Father asked. And Butcherknife Ike looked suddenly frightened, glancing sideways.

"No! No!" he said. "I'll go back there."

And when he learned that we had been as far down as Split Mountain Canyon and knew some of the country he had talked about, he seemed dismayed, as if afraid he had talked too much.

I last saw Butcherknife Ike about 1923. He had gone up San Juan Bautista Canyon, apparently heading for the desert. It was August and bitterly hot.

For some reason Father was a little worried about him, and suggested we take a lunch and go up the canyon. We found Butcherknife Ike at what used to be called Reed's Meadow, about eleven miles up from Morningside, on the bench before you climb into the high mountains. And he said that he was going through Coahuila and down Coyote Canyon and through Borrego Valley into the badlands. Someone had given him a book which told about the badlands being an unmined reservoir of rich minerals. So that's where he set his mind on going - and he picked the hottest week of the year. I took a picture of him and his burros. He went on. He never came back.

In spite of his queerness, the other prospectors that came and went had a great kindness for him. They went down and searched for him and asked about him. He had been seen at Borrego. He had gone into the badlands from there. But that was the end of the trail.

Artist's Rendition of a ship in the Desert
From the internet, no source given, no artist or copyright information

Butcherknife Ike, built a fire on a sand dune
in the desert, and found timbers of an old ship.

The Story of the Pearl Ship
by O. J. Fisk

In the year 1610 a contract was signed between the King of Spain and one Captain Thomas Cardona, whereby Cardona was authorized to engage in naval exploration and pearl hunting for the Crown, on both the Atlantic and Pacific oceans. Francisco Basilio was placed in charge of the Pacific division of the enterprise, but it was his great misfortune to die before the project was more than started. In Basilio's place, Cardona's nephew, Nicolas Cardona was placed, to take joint command with Juan de Iturbe and Sgt. Pedro Alvarez Rosales. Three ships were constructed in Acapulco, and after some delay they set sail from that port on March 21, 1615. Voyaging north, it is recorded that they took note of the rich mineral prospects with an eye to future development. They landed at 27 degrees latitude, finding relics of the Viscaino expedition, in the form of five Christian skulls and the fragments of a boat. Here they were attacked by a large party of hostile Indians; and Cardona was seriously wounded. It was decided that he should take one of the ships and return to Acapulco.

After Cardona turned back, Juan de Iturbe and Rosales sailed on in the other two vessels in the face of bad weather and food shortage, for the negro divers were eminently successful in their pearling activities. Iturbe also found it profitable to trade with the natives for pearls, giving old clothes and wormy ship's biscuit in return. The latter was highly regarded by the Indians, bringing a correspondingly higher price if the biscuit was so maggoty that it was fairly able to stand on its own feet, as it was then considered in the light of fresh meat.

From some unaccountable reason, our source of information at this point becomes rather vague as to just what happened to Rosales. We are able however to follow the activities of Iturbe. He sailed up the gulf, finding that it narrowed as he went, but finally opening up into what appeared to be a vast sea extending far inland. He was greatly excited, believing that he had found the fabled Straights of Anian, so long sought by the mariners of all countries, which would provide a passage between the two oceans.

However after many abortive attempts to find a way through he was at last forced to admit his defeat. He was however enabled to arrive at his approximate location, which was 34 degrees latitude (a fact which seems to me of very great significance, given that the present day Gulf of California does not extend above 32 degrees.) After many attempts to find a way out, he turned south once more only to find to his complete consternation that he was landlocked.

Frantically Iturbe sailed around the hemmed-in sea, seeking some exit. But his voyage came to an abrupt end when he grounded again and the water receding magically left him high and dry. He and his crew were forced to leave the ship with its vast treasure of pearls intact, realizing if they escaped with their lives alone they would be fortunate.

Iturbe's actions at this stage of the account become shrouded in obscurity. It may be that he was able to contact Rosales' ship. At any rate he next turned up at Sinaloa, where he build a new ship and made another pearling voyage.

Did Iturbe make an attempt to recover the vast cargo of pearls he was forced to leave with the abandoned ship? One chronicler, Ortega, records that only 14 marks of pearls were registered at the conclusion of the expedition, although Ortega states that he, personally, saw many times that number in Iturbe's possession. However, it is extremely doubtful if Iturbe ever made any attempt to return to his ship. We may safely conclude that the brooding sand dunes of "the land of little shells" still retain that "king's ransom" of pearls as well as the secret of the lost ship of the desert.

(From O.J. Fisk's "Story of the Pearl Ship of the Desert," Pioneer Cabin News, the San Bernadino Society of California Pioneers, Nov. 1951 to April 1952.)

A Dark Sky Over Death Valley
Credit: Dan Duriscoe, U.S. National Park Service

The Desert Ship
by the San Bernadino Guardian, October 15, 1870

The exploring party which left town some two seeks since for the purpose of examining the hull of a vessel said to be stranded in the Colorado Desert, has returned. All the members of the expedition are highly pleased with the result. Though they found no ship nor any sign thereof, yet they seem fully persuaded of the existence of some vessel.

Leaving Martinez, our friends plunged into the desert by the 'old road', abandoning the only traveled road, that of Dos Palmas, which deflects to the left. After thus leaving the road, the party traveled as far as possible. Indeed, they went until a glance backward showed them their footprints and the tracks of the wagon-wheels filled with water. Then they very naturally took fright and returned. As to the existence of a ship or something bearing a strong likeness to a ship, there can be no doubt. It is supposed to be stranded just southward of the point of the mountain southeast of Martinez.

That it will be found and the whole mystery solved admits of no doubt whatever. It is only a question of time, as a portion of the same party will start out in a few days to make another effort.

It is known that several vessels engaged in the expeditions to the Gulf of California have been lost; it is most likely that the hull now sought was one of these. Were it certain that the buccaneers had lost the vessel there would be an almost absolute certainty of rich booty, but the vessels sent out on voyages of discovery by the Viceroy of Mexico were generally very poorly freighted, yet they make up almost entirely the number of lost ships. A theory is maintained that the proper way to reach the ship is by way of the New River Station on the Ft. Yuma road, and this seems very probable. Turning north from New River Station, and passing the mud volcanoes, one would reach a point corresponding with that where the wreck must be situated. But after all, there is much that is visionary connected with the whole theory. It may be that what we call a ship may be a coral, as it has borne the appearance of one to one of the only two white men who have ever seen it. Yet let us hope that our desert holds some relic of the past history which may reveal to our enquiring eyes some lost mystery.

From the San Bernadino Guardian, December 3, 1870

In our last week's paper we chronicled the return of Charlie Clusker from a three to four week's 'cruise' in search of the desert ship, also the fact of his having been successful in finding it after days of faithful perseverance, and undergoing many severe hardships, in which he came near to losing his life, by perishing on the desert. But for all the hardships he endured he was repaid at last by finding the 'long lost' and much talked of vessel. It is now a fixed fact, for there can be no doubt but that the ship is lying high and dry, a hundred or two hundred miles from water, and the mystery which now hangs around it, will soon doubtless be cleared away.

On Wednesday morning last Mr. Clusker and party (four in all) started out to return to the ship. They are well fitted out with all necessary tools and implements, for thoroughly exploring the vessel, such as shovels, picks, blocks, chains, rope, and three or four hundred feet of boards. From this place they go to Warner's Ranch, and from that point direct for the ship. At Cariso Creek station, on the San Diego road, they intend making a depot for supplies, which will preclude the possibility of their suffering for food or water. We expect to receive some interesting news, from the party, in a week or two; may not however until their return to San Bernadino, when the mystery concerning the desert ship will be revealed. To those who are overanxious and curious to know how she came there and where she was going, we say, keep quiet and don't become excited, our associate in the Guardian, Mr. J.A. Talbott, is one of the party, and on his return will give no doubt an interesting description of the trip and the ship.

The Giants of Death Valley

Ancient Civilization Beneath Death Valley?
by The San Diego Union

**Expedition Reports
Nine-Foot Skeletons
August 4, 1947 edition of the
San Diego Union.**

According to the clipping, explorers had unearthed, near the Arizona-Nevada-California line, the mummified remains of strangely costumed giants which the discoverers dated to around 80,000 years ago.

The Union reported that a Howard E. Hill of Los Angeles was recounting the work of Dr. F. Bruce Russell, a retired Cincinnati physician who had originally located the first of several tunnels near Death Valley in 1931, but had not been able to return to the area until 1947.

With the help of Dr. Daniel S. Bovee, who with Hill's father had once helped open up New Mexico's cliff dwellings, Russell had recovered the remains of several men of 8 to 9 feet in height.

"These giants," said Hill, "are clothed in garments consisting of a medium length jacket and trouser extending slightly below the knees. The texture of the material is said to resemble gray dyed sheepskin, but obviously it was taken from an animal unknown today."

Hill also said, according to the Union, that in another cavern was found the ritual hall of the ancient people, together with devices and

Trace of Giants Found in Desert

LOS ANGELES, Aug. 4 (AP)—A retired Ohio doctor has discovered relics of an ancient civilization, whose men were 8 or 9 feet tall, in the Colorado desert near the Arizona-Nevada-California line, an associate said today.

Howard E. Hill, of Los Angeles, speaking before the Transportation Club, disclosed that several well-preserved mummies were taken yesterday from caverns in an area roughly 180 miles square, extending through much of southern Nevada from Death Valley, Calif., across the Colorado River into Arizona.

Hill said the discoverer is Dr. F. Bruce Russell, retired Cincinnati physician, who stumbled on the first of several tunnels in 1931, soon after coming West and deciding to try mining for his health.

MUMMIES FOUND

Not until this year, however, did Dr. Russell go into the situation thoroughly, Hill told the luncheon. With Dr. Daniel S. Bovee, of Los Angeles—who with his father helped open up New Mexico's cliff dwellings—Dr. Russell has found mummified remains together with implements of the civilization, which Dr. Bovee had tentatively placed at about 80,000 years old.

"These giants are clothed in garments consisting of a medium length jacket and trouser extending slightly below the knees," said Hill. "The texture of the material is said to resemble gray dyed sheepskin, but obviously it was taken from an animal unknown today."

MARKINGS DISCOVERED

Hill said that in another cavern was found the ritual hall of the ancient people, together with devices and markings similar to those now used by the Masonic order. In a long tunnel were well-preserved remains of animals, including elephants and tigers. So far, Hill added, no women have been found.

He said the explorers believe that what they found was the burial place of the tribe's hierarchy. Hieroglyphics, he added, bear a resemblance to what is known of those from the lost continent of Atlantis. They are chiseled, he added, on carefully-polished granite.

He said Dr. Viola V. Pettit, of London, who made excavations around Petra, on the Arabian desert, soon will begin an inspection of the remains.

markings similar to those now used by the Masonic order. In a long tunnel were well-preserved remains of animals, including elephants and tigers. So far, Hill added, no women have been found.

He said the explorers believe that what they found was the burial place of the tribe's hierarchy. Hieroglyphics, he added, bear a resemblance to what is known of those from the lost continent of Atlantis. They are chiseled, he added, on carefully polished granite.

Text of the Article:
TRACE OF GIANTS FOUND IN DESERT

LOS ANGELES, Aug 4. (AP)-- A retired Ohio doctor has discovered relics of an ancient civilization, whose men were 8 or 9 feet tall in the Colorado desert near the Arizona-Nevada-California line, an associate said today.

Howard E. Hill. of Los Angeles speaking before the Transportation Club, disclosed that several well-preserved mummies were taken yesterday from caverns in an area roughly 180 miles square, extending through much of southern Nevada from Death Valley, Calif. across the Colorado River into Arizona.

Hill said the discoverer is Dr. F. Bruce Russell, retired Cincinnati physician, who stumbled on the first of several tunnels in 1931, soon after coming West and deciding to try mining for his health.

MUMMIES FOUND

Not until this year, however, did Dr. Russell go into the situation thoroughly, Hill told the luncheon. With Dr. Daniel S. Bovee, of Los Angeles -- who with his father helped open up New Mexico's cliff dwellings -- Dr. Russell has found mummified remains together with implements of the civilization, which Dr. Bovee had tentatively placed at about 80,000 years old.

"These giants are clothed in garments consisting of a medium length jacket and trouser extending slightly below the knees." said Hill. "The texture of the material is said to resemble gray dyed sheepskin, but obviously it was taken from an animal unknown today."

MARKINGS DISCOVERED

Hill said that in another cavern was found the ritual hall of the ancient people, together with devices and markings similar to those now used by the Masonic order. In a long tunnel were well-preserved remains of animals including elephants and tigers. So far, Hill added, no women have been found.

He said the explorers believe that what they found was the burial place of the tribe's hierarchy. Hieroglyphics, he added, bear a resemblance to what is known of those from the lost continent of Atlantis. They are chiseled, he added, on carefully-polished granite.

He said Dr. Viola V. Pettit, of London, who made excavations around Petra, on the Arabian desert, soon will begin an inspection of the remains.

AN ABANDONED MILL.
In Death Valley

Second Article Concerning Same Discovery Of Giants and Caverns

Expedition Reports Nine-Foot Skeletons by the "Hot Citizen" Nevada Paper

August 5, 1947.

Death Valley

A band of amateur archaeologists announced today they have discovered a lost civilization of men nine feet tall in Californian caverns. Howard E. Hill, spokesman for the expedition, said the civilization may be "the fabled lost continent of Atlantis".

The caves contain mummies of men and animals and implements of a culture 80,000 years old but "in some respects more advanced than ours," Hill said. He said the 32 caves covered a 180-square-mile area in California's Death Valley and southern Nevada.

ARCHAEOLOGISTS SKEPTICAL

"This discovery may be more important than the unveiling of King Tut's tomb," he said. Professional archaeologists were skeptical of Hill's story. Los Angeles County Museum scientists pointed out that dinosaurs and tigers which Hill said lay side by side in the caves appeared on Earth 10,000,000 to 13,000,000 years apart.

Hill said the caves were discovered in 1931 by Dr F. Bruce Russell, Beverly Hills physician, who literally fell in while sinking a shaft for a mining claim.

"He tried for years to interest people in them," Hill said, "but nobody believed him." Russell and several hobbyists incorporated after the war as Amazing Explorations, Inc. and started digging. Several caverns contained mummified remains of "a race of men eight to nine feet tall," Hill said.

"They apparently wore a prehistoric zoot suit--a hair garment of medium length, jacket and knee-length trousers."

CAVERN TEMPLE FOUND

Another cavern contained their ritual hall with devices and markings similar to the Masonic order, he said. "A long tunnel from this temple took the party into a room where," Hill said, "well-preserved remains of dinosaurs, saber-toothed tigers, imperial elephants and other extinct beasts were paired off in niches as if on display.

"Some catastrophe apparently drove the people into the caves," he said. "All of the implements of their civilization were found," he said, "including household utensils and stoves which apparently cooked by radio waves."

"I know," he said, "that you won't believe that."

Article Concerning Same Cave Discovery by Different Men 10 to 15 Years Earlier

Ancient Civilization Beneath Death Valley?
Author unknown

Bourke Lee, in his book 'DEATH VALLEY MEN' (MacMillan Co., N.Y. 1932), chapter: "Old Gold", describes a conversation which he had several years ago with a small group of Death valley residents.

The conversation had eventually turned to the subject of Paihute Indian legends. At one point two of the men, Jack and Bill, described their experience with an 'underground city' which they claimed to have discovered after one of them had fallen through the bottom of an old mine shaft near Wingate Pass.

They found themselves in a natural underground cavern which they claimed to have followed about 20 miles north into the heart of the Panamint Mountains. To their amazement, they allegedly found themselves in an huge, ancient, underground cavern city.

They claimed that they discovered within the city several perfectly preserved 'mummies', which wore thick arm bands, wielded gold spears, etc. The city had apparently been abandoned for ages, except for the mummies, and the entire underground system looked very ancient.

It was formerly lit, they found out by accident, by an ingenious system of lights fed by subterranean gases. They claimed to have seen a large, polished round table which looked as if it may have been part of an ancient council chamber, giant statues of solid gold, stone vaults and drawers full of gold bars and gemstones of all kinds, heavy stone wheelbarrows which were perfectly balanced and scientifically-constructed so that a child could use them, huge stone doors which were almost perfectly balanced by counter-weights, and other incredible sights.

They also claimed to have followed the caverns upwards to a higher level which ultimately opened out onto the face of the Panamints, about half-way up the eastern slope, in the form of a few ancient tunnel-like quays.

They realized that the valley below was once under water and they eventually came to the conclusion that the arched openings were ancient 'docks' for sea vessels. They could allegedly see Furnace Creek Ranch and Wash far below them.

They told Bourke Lee that they had brought some of the treasure out of the caverns and tried to set up a deal with certain people, including scientists associated with the Smithsonian Institute, in order to gain help to explore and publicize the city as one of the 'wonders of the world'.

Furnace Creek and Wash

These efforts ended in disappointment however when a 'friend' of theirs stole the treasure (which was also the evidence) and they were scoffed at and rejected by the scientists when they went to show them the 'mine' entrance and could not find it.

A recent cloud-burst, they claimed, had altered and rearranged the entire countryside and the landscape did not look like it had been before.

When Lee last heard from the two men, Bill and Jack, they were preparing to climb the east face of the Panamints to locate the ancient tunnel openings or quays high up the side of the steep slope. Bourke Lee never did see or hear from his friends ever again.

In 1946 a man calling himself Dr. F. Bruce Russell, and claiming to be a retired physician, told a similar story about finding strange underground rooms in the Death Valley area in 1931.

He told of a large room with several tunnels leading off in different directions. One of these tunnels led to another large room that contained three mummies.

Artifacts found in the room appeared to be a combination of Egyptian and American Indian design. The most amazing thing about the mummies though was the fact that they were more than eight feet tall.

Dr. Russell and a group of investors formed "Amazing Explorations, Inc" to handle the release, and profit, from this remarkable find. But, as stories of this type usually go, Russell disappeared, and the investigators were never able to find the caverns and tunnels again, even though Russell had personally taken them there.

The desert can be very deceiving to anyone not used to traveling it. Month's later, Russell's car was found abandoned, with a burst radiator, in a remote area of Death Valley. His suitcase was still in the car.

The old TV series Death Valley Days once ran a short story about western pioneers also finding mummies in the desert. Since one of the script writers stated that "there had never been a script without a solid basis in fact", it would be interesting to find out what their source had been.

For now, these stories will have to be shrouded in mystery, along with the 21,000 year old bones found in California's Imperial Valley, also rumored to have been spirited off by the Smithsonian.

Source: Shadowlands Underworld

RESIDENCE OF F. M. SMITH, TEELS, MARCH, 1873.
Desert Homestead

San Bernardino Caves - Kokoweef Caverns Sworn Statement Of E. P. Dorr.

Below you will find a transcription of the sworn statement made by Earl Dorr as it pertained to Kokoweef Caverns. This was published in the California Mining Journal, November 1940, though written in 1934.

It is speculated that Earl was attempting to get capital at the time for his projects in the area.

TO WHOM IT MAY CONCERN:

This is to certify that there is located in San Bernardino County, California, about two hundred and fifty miles from Los Angeles, a certain cave.

Traveling over state highways by automobile, the cave is reached in about ten hours.

A Civil Engineer, Mr. Morton, and I spent four days exploring the cave for more than eight miles. We carried with us Altimeters, Pedometers, and a Theodolite, with which to observe and record actual directions, take elevations and measurements by triangulation. Our exploration revealed the following facts:

1. From the mouth of the cave we descended as shown by the Altimeters to be about 2000 feet, where we encountered a canyon, which from the Altimeters and by calculations we found to be from 3000 to 3500 feet deeper; making total depth of 5400 feet from the mouth where we entered the caves to the floor of the canyon.

2. We found the cave divided into many caverns or chambers, of various sizes, all filled and embellished with Stalactites and Stalagmites, besides many grotesque and fantastic shapes that make these caves one of the wonders of the world.

3. The largest chamber we explored is about 300 ft. wide, 400 feet long and from 50 to 110 feet high. It is encrusted with crystals, fashioned into festoons of innumerable Stalactites, that hang from the ceiling, some of which are extremely large.

4. One, the largest seen, is 27 feet in diameter and hangs 1510 feet down into a 3000 ft. canyon. This great Stalactite is perpetually washed by water flowing down over it and falling into the dark canyon depths. The huge glistening white crystal is 500 feet longer than the Eiffel Tower, and challenged us with amazement and wonder.

5. There is a flowing river on the floor of the canyon, which rises and falls with tidal regularity. All measurements and estimates of the river, including its tides and beach sands were reckoned by triangulation, taken with the Theodolite, and while we did not reach the river, nevertheless, taking observations with our theodolite and its telescope, we reckoned the river to be about 300 feet wide at high tide and 10 feet wide at low tide. It rises and falls from 7 ½ to 8 feet. The Peysert brothers confirm our reckoning.

Photo showing the interior of Kokoweef Caverns.
Courtesy of Jack Russ.

6. When the tide is out, there is exposed on both sides of the river from 100 to 159 feet of black sand, which the Peysert brothers report is very rich in placer gold. They report the sands on the river shore to be from 4 to 11 feet deep; and on an average about 8 feet deep.

7. There are numerous ledges above the canyon that are from 10 to 40 feet wide and covered with sand. We personally explored the ledge sands for a distance of more than eight miles, finding little variation in the depth and width of these ledge sands. And wherever examined, the ledge sands are found to be fabulously rich in placer gold.

8. I have known intimately Oliver, Buck and George Peysert From my boyhood. I have discussed these caves with them repeatedly and thoroughly. They have reported to me in detail, their experience in exploring the caves.

One of them, George, lost his life in the cave. Buck and Oliver say George was killed by diving in the river on the floor of the canyon.

He struck an unseen rock, which killed him instantly. They have reported to me repeatedly their mining experiences and say they mined on the beach sands of the river a total in all of six weeks.

They carried lumber down to the river and constructed a sluice box and, using a pump, the three mined for six weeks, during which time they recovered more than $57,000 in gold, (gold at $20.00 per ounce); they sent their gold directly to the U.S. Mint and banked the returns in a bank in Needles, California, and another bank in Las Vegas, Nevada.

I last talked to them in my home about November 10th 1934, at which time they repeated their former statements, giving information as to how they discovered the river, and more of their experiences in gold mining. They recovered several of the largest nuggets of gold ever found in California.

Both Mr. Morton and myself filled our pockets with the sands from the ledges, carried it out and had it assayed. Just what Mr. Morton's sand assayed, I do not know, but it was approximately $2000. per ton.

I carried out ten pounds and two ounces of the ledge sand, and panned seven pounds, recovering more than $7.00 in gold, with gold at $20.00 an ounce. I sold the gold for $18.00 per ounce.

The balance of my ten pounds of sand I sent to John Herman, a Los Angeles Assayer. His assay certificate shows a value of $2,144.47 per yard - gold at $20.67 per ounce.

I, E. P. DORR residing at 300 Aldena Street, Pasadena California make the foregoing statements for the purpose of inducing investors to invest in the work of mining the gold in these caves, and solemnly swear that all statements made hereinabove are true and that all persons will find the physical conditions in the cave as above stated.

SUBSCRIBED and sworn to this ___ day of December, 1934

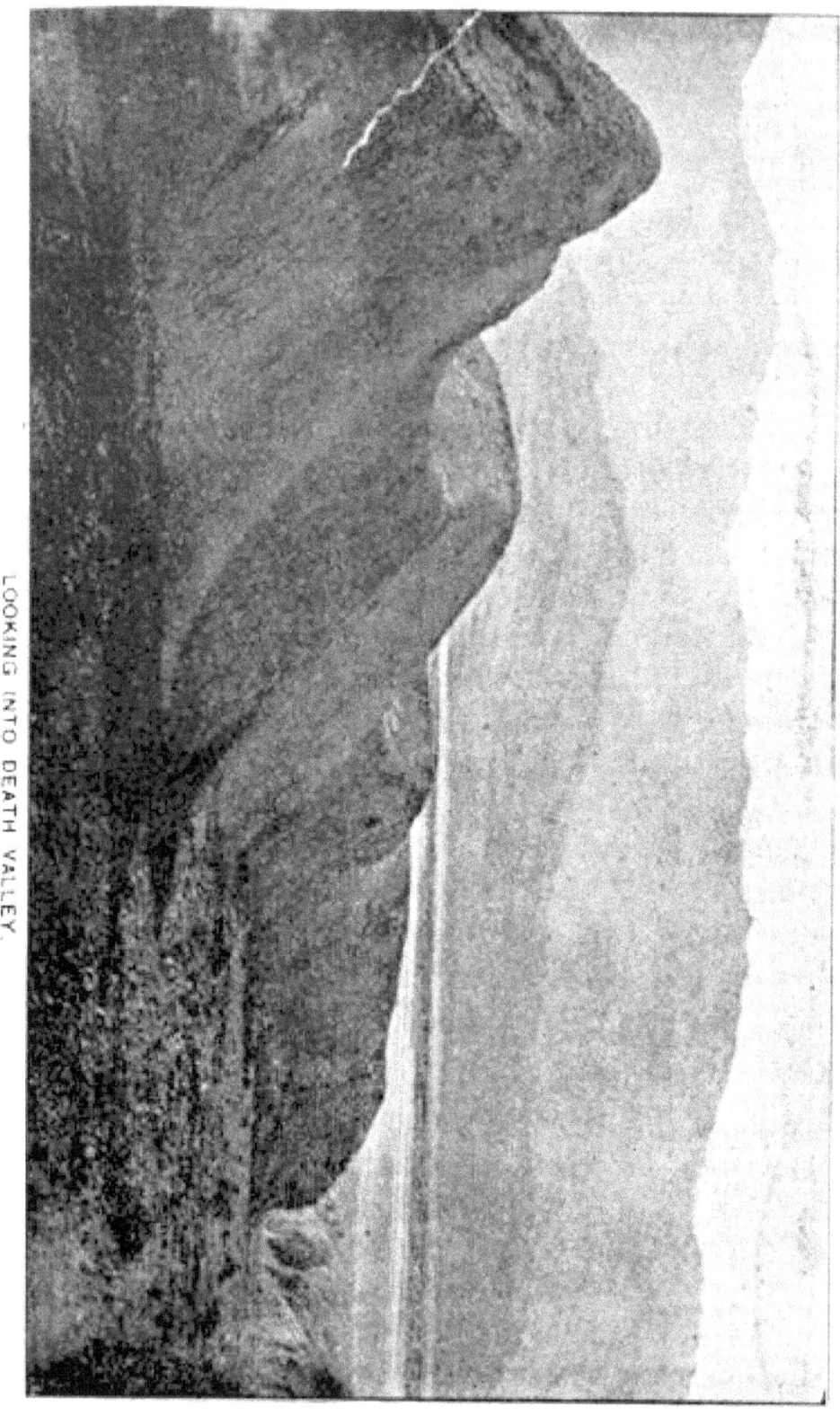
LOOKING INTO DEATH VALLEY.

Strange Alien Artifact Discovered In the Desert
by Timothy Green Beckley

While the rest of the nation was experiencing a cold snap that sent temperatures plunging well below freezing, Orlando was registering temperatures of 80 degrees, making it the warmest city anywhere in the entire country. I had already been in Florida for more than a week, making appearances on various TV and radio talk shows, promoting UFO REVIEW. While back in New York before venturing South after Christmas, I had received an urgent call from Karen Alt, a UFO REVIEW correspondent who has covered fast-breaking UFO stories in the past. This time her conversation had centered around an unusual "artifact" supposedly found at the site of a UFO crash. She had heard a remarkable story from a student attending Seminole Community College in nearby Sanford, where she works as a secretary. Realizing that UFO skeptics such as Philip Klass and NASA's James Oberg are always clamoring for "physical evidence," Karen was understandably excited over what she thought might be an important breakthrough in the field. She wanted to know if I'd be willing to talk with the person who owned the artifact and get the inside scoop.

Naturally, I was fascinated. However, I was determined to make certain this wasn't some type of crude hoax. After all, if this was the "real McCoy' and not a fraud, UFOlogists would at long last have something concrete to rub in the noses of the non-believers.

A three decades-long search for physical evidence that would conclusively prove that flying saucers are "somebody else's spacecraft," may have recently reached the exciting climax with the discovery of actual "hardware" from a crashed UFO.

The important discovery was made in late 1977 by an Orlando, Florida, health food store owner when jogging across the United States. While he was unable to carry all of what he found back across the country with him, John Peele now has in his possession what he maintains is a glove once worn by an alien astronaut that crashed to

Earth. Moreover, the owner of this glove—a glove that is far too small for any earthly pilot to wear—is confident that the entire craft which brought the alien to our planet is still under the sifting sands, just waiting to be retrieved at some future date.

A firm believer in physical fitness, John Peel and his wife Nancy, exercise daily and have adopted a strict vegetarian diet. In order to promote their particular lifestyle, the couple— along with their young son and a close friend — ran some 3,100 miles to call attention to the fact that jogging is healthy for the body and a perfect way to get (and remain) in shape.

They began their adventure over the 1977 Labor Day weekend, leaving Daytona, Florida and heading West. Their 91-day run took them through both large and small towns as well as along shores, through steaming deserts and over mountainous terrain.

A firm believer in physical fitness, John Peele found mysterious "alien glove" as he tracked across the desert. o this day, he's uncertain what his discovery indicates, but he is positive, the artifact is genuine.

For the most part, the weather was nearly perfect, making it possible for John to cover an appropriate distance during the daylight hours. Later, just before sunset, John and his jogging partner would join up with Nancy Peel and their son, who were driving ahead in a camper-van.

"We were preparing to leave El Centro, California, when a bad wind storm came up, toppling cars and semi's along I-10." John Peele began his extensive narrative as we sat in the living room of his nicely furnished, Spanish-style townhouse. "The wind was blowing upwards to 125 miles per hour and so we knew it would be foolish to think we could get any further that day.

"By the next morning, however, the sky had cleared and the day promised to be near excellent for jogging. We had headed out over the desert through the town of Ocotillo, a stone's throw from the Mexican border. The road we were running on quickly came to an end, and we soon started to cross what appeared to be an old, dried up river bed. Around the next bend was a railroad trestle that was almost totally demolished."

John admits that he isn't sure just how old the trestle was, or what a railroad was doing in this particular location. "The rails didn't look as if they were particularly old — they weren't rusty or anything — but the desert does tend to be deceiving, and the lack of rain in the area could have kept them looking relatively new, when, in reality, they might have dated back many years.

Keeping a slower than normal pace, John and his companion tried to run along the tracks. But the rails would buckle up and down in the desert making it difficult to jog without spraining an ankle in the twisted metal.

Leaving the track, they headed toward a mountain peak that loomed in the distance. At this point, John admits to feeling something "very odd" in the air. Suddenly, they were confronted by what appeared to be an aerial wreck of some sort.

"There, jutting up out of the desert, were several large pieces of what resembled Plexiglas." Having been an army helicopter pilot stationed in Viet Nam for over a year, John was positive they could not have been pieces from the windshield of a crashed Army or Air Force vehicle.

"First off, the material was a deep royal blue, not the color used in military windshields." John explained that to his knowledge, Phantom and Cobra helicopters use Plexiglas that is tinted light blue toward the top of the windshield to block out the harsh rays of the sun. "But this was much too dark to see through,' he continued. "The largest piece of this strange royal blue glass measured some two square feet. There were many other smaller pieces of two or three inches in diameter lying all over the place."

A little further on, something else on the ground caught his eye. "There was all this lightweight metal that felt similar to aluminum, except that it was smooth on one side, honeycombed on the other, and when I tried to bend it the metal wouldn't give."

Realizing that he had probably come across something highly unusual, John picked up several of the smaller pieces and put them into his pocket for safekeeping.

Yet this was not all he was to find. For there on the ground not far away was a glove not totally unlike the pressurized gloves worn by our high altitude test pilots and astronauts. What made John do a double-take was the fact that this pressurized glove was in miniature form as if it had been made for a child. Of course, children do not pilot high altitude planes, nor does the government allow individuals under a certain size to join the service, ruling out that the glove might have been manufactured for a midget.

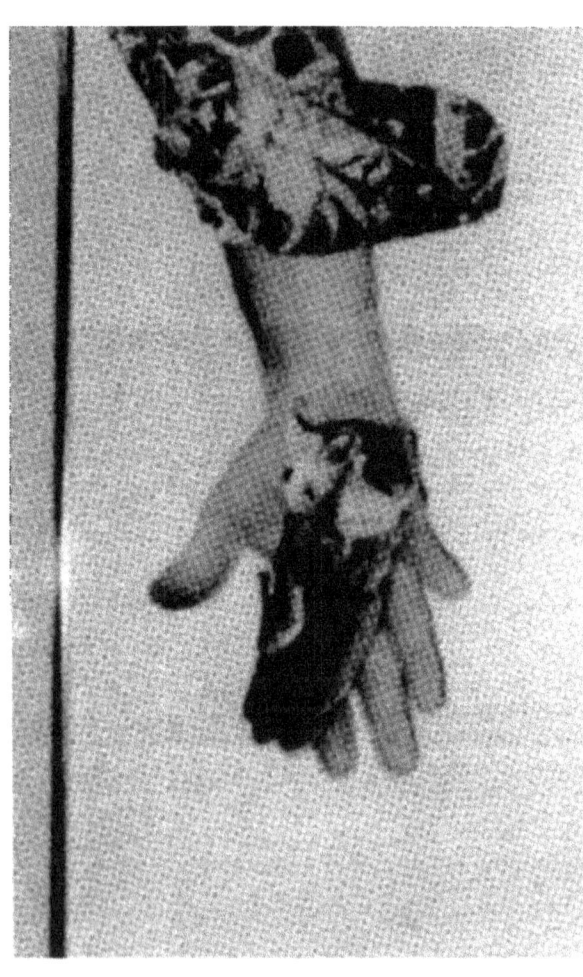

Author took these photos while visiting Peele. Note size of glove when held in the normal-size hand of a human.

Only a few feet away was a second glove, this one having apparently been burned in a crash. It was not in prefect condition like the other glove, having obviously been badly scorched by extreme heat.

While John held an intense curiosity about what he had found, his jogging partner did not share the same sense of discovery.

"You'd better drop that thing," he warned. "If it's radioactive, your hand will fall off."

Disturbed over what he considered to be a distinct possibility at the time, and realizing that they had already far too much to carry, John took the good glove, along with some pieces of the strange blue glass as well as the aluminum-like metal, and buried them.

"I found a natural cave under some rocks and placed everything carefully inside, expecting to return shortly and reclaim my findings.

Luckily, at the last minute, I decided to take the partly burned glove along with me, as I thought it might be relatively safe compared to the glove that was in perfect condition."

John placed markers around the area where he hid the items, so that the exact spot would be known to him when he returned in the future.

However, when he tried to reclaim his discovery, a peculiar storm came up, sending him scurrying out of the desert for safety.

"We were driving back after the last leg of our run. With my wife Nancy at the wheel, my jogging companion and my son in the back of the van, I joked about how when we got back to the cave there would probably be an alien guarding the spot.

"All of a sudden a tremendous storm came up out of nowhere. The sky turned pitch black as if it were in the middle of the night. Later, we talked to local residents who told us they couldn't remember the last time it stormed in this part of the desert."

As hard as it might be for him to accept, John can't help feel that "cosmic forces were at work," preventing him from returning to reclaim the good glove and the other artifacts. "I'm positive that it's still where I put it, and I can't help but believe that the remains of an entire ship that crashed is buried in the desert nearby." If this is the case, then this would definitely prove the validity of UFOs and would be the clincher in proving that alien beings are coming to Earth on a regular basis. In addition, being that the gloves have five fingers, this would indicate that their wearer was a humanoid similar to our own race of homo sapiens; except that they are probably smaller in stature, a factor often reported in the sighting of UFO occupants.

The return trip to Florida was uneventful, although John couldn't get over the nagging feeling that his discovery was earth shaking in its implications. In Healing Waters, Arizona, the party got additional confirmation that we are not the only individuals capable of flight.

"Overhead, late one night," Nancy Peele told UFO REVIEW, "we saw an object as bright as a street lamp zipping back and forth across the darkened sky. I watched it for over 35 minutes through the windshield of our van, and I was amazed at the way it would move from one part of the star-filled heavens to another, and then drop down before eventually shooting straight up into space."

Arriving back in the Orlando area, John remained excited over the one glove he still had with him. And while he never advertised that he owned such a strange artifact, he sealed the partially burned glove in a transparent pack and kept it under the counter of his newly opened 21st Century Health Food Store located in Winter Park. From time to time he would show it to customers, who would usually walk off after examining it, nodding their heads in total wonderment.

One of the things that was immediately noticed was the manner in which the glove was stitched. "It was double stitched, unlike anything of the type our military makes. Also, the stitching had not shrunk, despite the fact that it had quite obviously been exposed to a high temperature." Also, it was ascertained that the zipper of the glove seemed to zip from the inside, a most peculiar feature. The glove appears to be made out of a leather-like material, and is composed of three layers that have been peeled back partially, no doubt due to the nature of the crash the wearer of the glove had to go through. The alien glove is maybe half the size of a glove worn by a normal-sized human, and when compared to the size of paper money it is easy to see just how small the glove really is.

Without a doubt, the strangest feature is the stamping of the word "LARGE" in English on the innermost layer of material. Almost immediately one would assume that this would rule out the glove being of extraterrestrial origin. But, the fact remains that no pressurized glove of this size would ever be marked "LARGE" if it were manufactured by our military.

John has gone over all the possibilities in his mind and still comes up with a blank. "Someone suggested that the glove might have been worn by a monkey, since NASA did send several monkeys into space in the early days of our space program. However, this doesn't hold water either, since the thumb of a monkey is further down on its hand than the thumb on a man. Interestingly, the thumb of this glove is higher up, indicating an advanced species."

More questions pop up, but few answers have been forthcoming to date regarding John Peele's discovery. Understandably, because of its potential value, the glove's owner has been very reluctant to let the glove out of his sight. "One time I allowed someone from the Martin-Marietta Company, a firm with government connections that is responsible for the manufacture of parts in our guided missile systems, to take it out of the shop back to his firm to have it examined by scientists. He was convinced that I had come across something highly unusual. But once he had the glove in his hands, his attitude changed. He had promised to return it right away, and now I wasn't even able to get him to come to the phone. Finally, he sent it back without any type of analysis or even a letter.

"Representatives of Rockwell International as well as NASA have privately looked at the glove and have told me that to their knowledge the glove was not manufactured by any private contractor. Each time they come back to the peculiar stitching and the location of the thumb placement on the glove."

Of course, John is well aware of the value of what he accidentally came across in the California desert, but to date he hasn't had any luck profiting from his unique discovery.

"When the movie 'Close Encounters of the Third Kind' opened in Orlando, I introduced myself to the manager of the theater, telling him what I had and offering to put the glove on display in the theater for his patrons to examine in the lobby. He agreed that the artifact would be a good draw, but when I glove and showed it to him, the manager really 'freaked out' and refused to put it on exhibit. An assistant informed me later that he thought the glove would really frighten people who came in expecting to see a science fiction film."

John acknowledges that he is in no way opposed to having the glove examined by those who are competent to do so. But, on the other hand, he is quite familiar with the various ill-fated attempts to analyze what was thought to be physical evidence of a UFO that supposedly crashed in Brazil— the material under inspection having been "accidentally/' washed down the drain by a scientist involved in the inquiry.

John Peele is the first to admit he isn't completely certain what the extent of his discovery may be, but he is convinced that the glove is some sort of outer space artifact, and that furthermore, below the desert outside of a small California town, are the remains of a vehicle that carried a humanoid being to this planet. Perhaps the alien itself is still among the wreckage. Maybe he escaped. But, John Peele plans to eventually go back to the "crash site" and look for himself. What he uncovers could well be the most important discovery of all time and remember—where you read about it first.

Monument Valley - Utah Desert
Photo: Jon Sullivan

Ghost Camels of the Desert
by Joe Parzanse

Millions of years ago, camels roamed the North American continent. The camel family evolved here and migrated over into Africa and the Middle East as they slowly died out on this continent. One species of camel even persisted in California until only 15 thousand years ago. Today, old fossils and bones of these ancient camels are still found; as recently as October 2002 down in Long Beach.

But although these camels long died out, rumors, folklore, and legends in the American South West still tell tales of wild camels and even ghost camels wandering the deserts of California, Utah, Nevada, Arizona and Texas. Some attribute these sightings to remnants of the US Camel Corps put together back in the mid 1800's. Although how the camels could survive until today or if they have been reproducing in the wild is a mystery. A few states once had laws on the books preventing the use of camels on certain highways, a result of problems occurring with camel use shortly after the closure of the US Camel Corps. Nevada, for example, passed a law in February of 1875 prohibiting camels and dromedaries from running at large on public roads in the state. The act was repealed in 1899.

The US Camel Corps was a mid 19th century concept by the US Army put into motion ironically by future President of the Confederate States, Jefferson Davis. The idea was to find alternate means of transportation in the dry and rough climate of the South Western United States. To put the plan into motion $30,000 was set aside on March 3rd, 1855. Although it took awhile traveling the Middle East, the US eventually had 34 camels (give or take one or two, reports vary, although it is interesting to note that all reports state that at least one camel was born on the trip overseas back from Egypt) arrive in Texas late April of 1856. Several handlers from the Middle East were also brought with the camels. The most famous was a Syrian named Hadji Ali, although he was called Hi Jolly. A second later shipment brought the number of US camels up to 77.

The Red Ghost - Drawing by Jeff Hatch

Loading up a Camel in the Middle East

The camel corps first and really only use was by Lieutenant Beale who led many of the camels across the country to California. Although Beale pronounced the camel experiment a success, many had their doubts. The camels bit, spit, and kicked their American handlers and disrupted the local livestock with their smell. After their trial run, Beale put the camels up on his friend's ranch, claiming that they should stay in California for future use if a war with the Mormons of Utah ever occurred. His friend, Samuel Bishop utilized the camels to haul freight on his own ranch and back and forth to Fort Tejon. The route taken to Fort Tejon passed through lands controlled by the Mojave Indians who often attacked civilian transports, but avoided any military soldiers. As Bishop was a civilian and the camel experiment currently officially a civilian experiment, no soldiers were with the camel caravans traveling from Bishop's ranch to Fort Tejon. A large force of Mojave Indians threatened Bishop's teamsters, forcing Bishop to order them to mount the camels and charge the attackers. The surprise charge of the teamsters on such strange beasts did in fact rout the Mojave Indians and also went down in history as probably the only camel charge in the west, which ironically was performed by civilians as opposed to the military.

Edward Fitzgerald Beale (1822-1893)

There are rumors of a few more experiments performed with the camels. They are attributed to the US army when it was still trying to find a use for the beasts. The first involved using the camels in an attempt to perform a pony express or "camel express". Sadly in both the first and second attempt the camel dropped dead from exhaustion. It was determined that although the camel could carry enormous loads and travel for extended periods of time with little rest, food, or water, it was not an appropriate steed for a mailman to speedily deliver the mail, especially since its maximum speed appeared to be no faster than the mules already used to deliver the mail. In the second experiment, the army turned the camels over to a survey crew, mapping the Nevada / California border. The expedition became lost, was forced to abandon their equipment, lost their mules, and grew hopeless of ever surviving to see civilization. The camels took over the mission, led the crew back to Visalia, and saved the surveyors.

Regardless of how well the camels did or did not perform, the coming of the Civil War pretty much put an end to the camel experiment and doomed the US Camel Corps. Although it is interesting to note, that at least the Confederate side, and maybe even the Union side, captured camels from the other during the war. Also, it is rumored that as the Civil War was breaking out, the Secretary of War was urging Congress to allow the purchase of 1000 more camels for use in the American Southwest. Despite their successes or lack their of, and the backing of people such as the Secretary of War, the Civil War and the laying of more railroads that followed killed the U.S. Camel Corps.

The California camels traveled from Fort Tejon to the Los Angeles Quartermaster Office and finally to Benicia. By November 1863, the California Camels were put up for sale and purchased largely by zoos, circuses, and mining operations with a few camels going to private individuals such as Beale himself. Those camels remaining in Texas were sold off in 1865, though the government later reclaimed some of them as stolen property and then promptly released them into the desert on their own.

Many of the mining operations often later released the camels into the wild when they either served no further need for them or grew tired of the camels biting, kicking, and spitting at their owners. These released camels wandered the deserts with confirmed sightings until the early 1900s. Although to this day, several people still claim the camels survive in remote areas of the US Southwest.

The most interesting story about the camels is that of the Red Ghost. Depending on who you talk to, the legend goes something like this. A young recruit in the army was having difficulty learning how to ride the camels. To teach him a lesson and to get him to no longer be afraid of the camels, they tossed him on top of one and lashed him to the beast. Then they smacked the camel and began chasing after it as it dashed off in fright. The camel, later dubbed the Red Ghost, easily out paced the other camels and riders, escaping into the desert with the poor army soldier still helplessly tied to it, never to be seen again.

The story continues in 1883, when a woman was said to be found trampled by a large beast. Bits of red fur were found at the scene. Several other sightings occurred afterwards all leaving large hoof prints, and a rancher reported that the creature had a rider. Supposedly some prospectors eventually sighted the creature and saw something fall from its back. That something was apparently a human skull. For years, the camel terrorized the countryside and eventually in 1893, the Red Ghost, now with its headless rider was killed by an Arizona farmer. The rider had long ago fallen off leaving only leather straps behind on the camel. To this day, however, every once in awhile stories of a giant red camel with a white stripe down its side (the leg bones of the corpse still strapped to it) appear. The Red Ghost has apparently gone spiritual and still haunts the deserts of the American Southwest.

Hi Jolly, one of the camel handlers, tried running a freighting business with some of the camels, but that sadly failed and he also eventually released his camels into the wild. He eventually died at age 73 in December 1902 in Arizona. A pyramid shaped monument was erected for him in Quartzsite, Arizona. One account has him dying a year later chasing after the Red Ghost. This story has Hi Jolly's withered body found, arms wrapped around the neck of the corpse of the great red camel.

An exhibit / museum at Fort Irwin out near Barstow discusses Hi Jolly and the Camel Corps. The exhibit features a real stuffed camel, although not one of Hi Jolly's original camels. The exhibit explains how Hi Jolly once saved five Americans from an Indian attack by charging them on his camel, cloak billowing out behind him, waving his scimitar yelling out 'Bismiallah' or "God is Great". The Indians had never seen a camel or a rider like Hi Jolly and turned and fled. Supposedly the exhibit also contains two Philippine combs that use to be dipped in poison and a Philippine Poking Device which is a human leg bone that you'd poke your enemy with. Fort Irwin handles training the U.S. military for combat with enemy nationalities. It simulates real Iraq villages to get soldiers ready for Middle Eastern urban combat. Additionally, Fort Irwin holds Goldstone. Goldstone houses multiple satellite dishes used by JPL and NASA as part of their Deep Space Network. These satellite dishes receive transmissions from many of the probes, satellites and rovers that NASA and other governments have spread across the galaxy.

Two other herds of camels were reportedly brought into the US around the time of the US Camel Corps. One in 1858, the other in 1859, and both I believe in Texas. Both shipments, however, were really slave ships trying to use the camel smell to cover up the odor typically associated with a slave ship. After being detained at port, both ships dumped off their camels on the docks and set sail for more slave friendly nations. The camels were pretty much left to their own devices, many either ending up shot or escaping out of town and into the wilderness beyond.

Other camels were brought into San Francisco in 1860 for work in Nevada. And another shipment arrived in the state in 1862, although they were quickly resold to British Columbia.

Camels do still reside in California today. In San Diego California, Oasis Camel Dairy claims to be America's first and only camel dairy. They currently make and offer six different flavors of Camel Milk Soap. Also there are occasionally Camel races at several state fairs. The bones of one of the original camels from the Camel Corps still exists at the Smithsonian Museum of Natural History. The camel, originally named Seid was killed by another camel named Tuili, but thankfully its remains were shipped back to Washington DC by a man named Sylvester Mowry where they still sit today.

Today, rumors still persist that camels exist in the deserts of California, Arizona, and Nevada. Some attribute this to reclusive descendants of the original camels long ago released. Others attribute it to the ghosts of those released, silently wandering the desert in stoic lines. Are there camels still living in the deserts of the American West? Or are people just seeing their ghosts?

But if you're out driving down the long lonely highways of California's deserts, and you think, out of the corner of your eye, that you've seen a camel, pause for a second, for you just might have seen one. Then again maybe it was the Red Ghost still haunting the deserts of California.

Jake's Camels

One other story about the camels involves a prospector named Jake who purchased three camels from the army in San Francisco. The story goes on to state how although the camels were foul beasts that spit, kicked, and bit many of the people in the town including Jake, Jake cared for them and spoke nothing but praise about them.

Eventually Jake made a big gold strike, and came into town with his camels' saddlebags over flowing with gold. Later that night, after Jake had celebrated his find at the local tavern, a man called Paul Adams followed him and murdered him. But Jake had been smart and hadn't gone back to the location of the mine. Additionally one of his camels had attacked the murderer, and had unfortunately been shot and killed as well, but not before taking a good bite out of Paul. A dark bit of cloth was found clutched in the camel's dead mouth.

Paul was unable to located the missing mine, but Jake's ghost and the ghost of the camel found him. Jake and his spectral mount came riding up one night and chased Adams through town right up to the sheriff. After Paul Adams gave a confession, the ghosts of both Jake and the dead camel faded away.

The Story goes on to say that Jake appeared one final time to give the location of the mine and his remaining two camels to one of his friends.

Credit: www.WeirdCa.com

Meteor Crater
Meteor Crater is one of the youngest and best-preserved impact craters on Earth. The crater formed roughly 50,000 years ago when a 30-meter-wide, iron-rich meteor weighing 100,000 tons struck the Arizona desert at an estimated 20 kilometers per second. The resulting explosion exceeded the combined force of today's nuclear arsenals and created a 1.1-kilometer-wide, 200-meter-deep crater.
Text & Photo NASA

The Racetrack
by U.S. National Park Service

Nestled in a remote valley between the Cottonwood and Last Chance Ranges, the Racetrack is a place of stunning beauty and mystery. The Racetrack is a playa--a dry lakebed--best known for it's strange moving rocks. Although no one has actually seen the rocks move, the long meandering tracks left behind in the mud surface of the playa attest to their activity.

Racetrack Playa is located in a high valley in the Cottonwood Mountains of the Panamint Range. The playa is in one of the most remote regions of the park accessible only by the rugged, typically washboard-ridden unpaved Racetrack Road and two other longer 4-wheel drive roads over Hunter Mountain or through Saline Valley. (Grandstand at bottom of mountains) Photo: usgs.gov

Ubehebe Craters include over a dozen volcanoes formed from great blasts of steam, rock, and volcanic tuff and ash when rising magma came in contact with water filled alluvial fan sediments on the north side of Tin Mountain. The near lack of erosion and lack of soil on Ubehebe Crater (shown here) suggests that the last eruption was less than 10,000 years ago. Photo: usgs.gov

Racetrack Road

The road to Racetrack Valley begins near Ubehebe Crater. Normally it is recommended for high-clearance vehicles as it can be rough and washboard. Off-road driving is prohibited as the desert is very fragile and vehicle tracks can remain for years. Watch for Joshua trees along the way. Often confused with cactus, Joshua trees actually are a type of yucca that can grow up to 30 feet tall. Twenty miles in you will reach Teakettle Junction. Follow the road straight ahead to the Racetrack playa. The road to the left leads into Hidden Valley and connects with the Hunter Mountain road which usually requires 4- wheel-drive to travel. Two miles further the short spur road to the right leads to the Ubehebe Lead Mine. It operated during the late 1800's and again during World War I.

Leadfield is a ghost town along Titus Canyon Drive. The town was established as a hoax silver claim. The town promoter, C. C. Julian, blasted some tunnels and salted them with lead ore he had brought from Nevada. He then lured Eastern investors, miners, and other hopefuls to move to his new town, and even conned the U.S. Government to build a post office. For six months over between August, 1926 and February, 1927, over 300 people tried to make a strike, but they never found anything but traces of ore. The post office closed, and the town's people vanished, leaving behind a few holes and ruined shacks. Photo: usgs.gov

The Teakettle Junction sign (with a constantly changing array of teakettles) is located at the junction of backcountry roads: the Racetrack Road and Hunter Mountain Road (Hidden Valley Road) in the Cottonwood Mountains about 18 miles south of Ubehebe Crater. Photo: usgs.gov

Grandstand

After traveling 26 miles you reach the north end of the Racetrack and the Grandstand parking area. A short walk out to the Grandstand can be rewarding. This large island outcrop of quartz monzonite offers spectacular views of the Racetrack. Those interested in a longer hike should try the old miner's trail to Ubehebe Peak. This strenuous 6 mile round trip hike involves an elevation gain of 1800 feet. Look for this trail west of the Grandstand parking lot. The Racetrack is a playa (dry lakebed) about 3 miles long and 2 miles wide. At least 10,000 years ago this region underwent climatic changes resulting in cycles of hot, cold and wet periods. As the climate changed, the lake evaporated and left behind beige colored mud, at least 1,000 feet thick.

The Grandstand, Photos: Manoseca

Moving Rocks

To see the moving rocks, drive two miles south of the Grandstand parking area. Walk at least a half mile toward the southeast corner of the playa for the best views of rocks and their tracks on the playa. Erosional forces cause rocks from the surrounding mountains to tumble to the surface of the Racetrack. Once on the floor of the playa the rocks move across the level surface leaving trails as records of their movements. Some of the moving rocks are large and have traveled as far as 1,500 feet. Throughout the years many theories have been suggested to explain the mystery of these rock movements. A research project has suggested that a rare combination of rain and wind conditions enable the rocks to move. A rain of about 1/2 inch, will wet the surface of the playa, providing a firm but extremely slippery surface. Strong winds of 50 mph or more, may skid the large boulders along the slick mud.

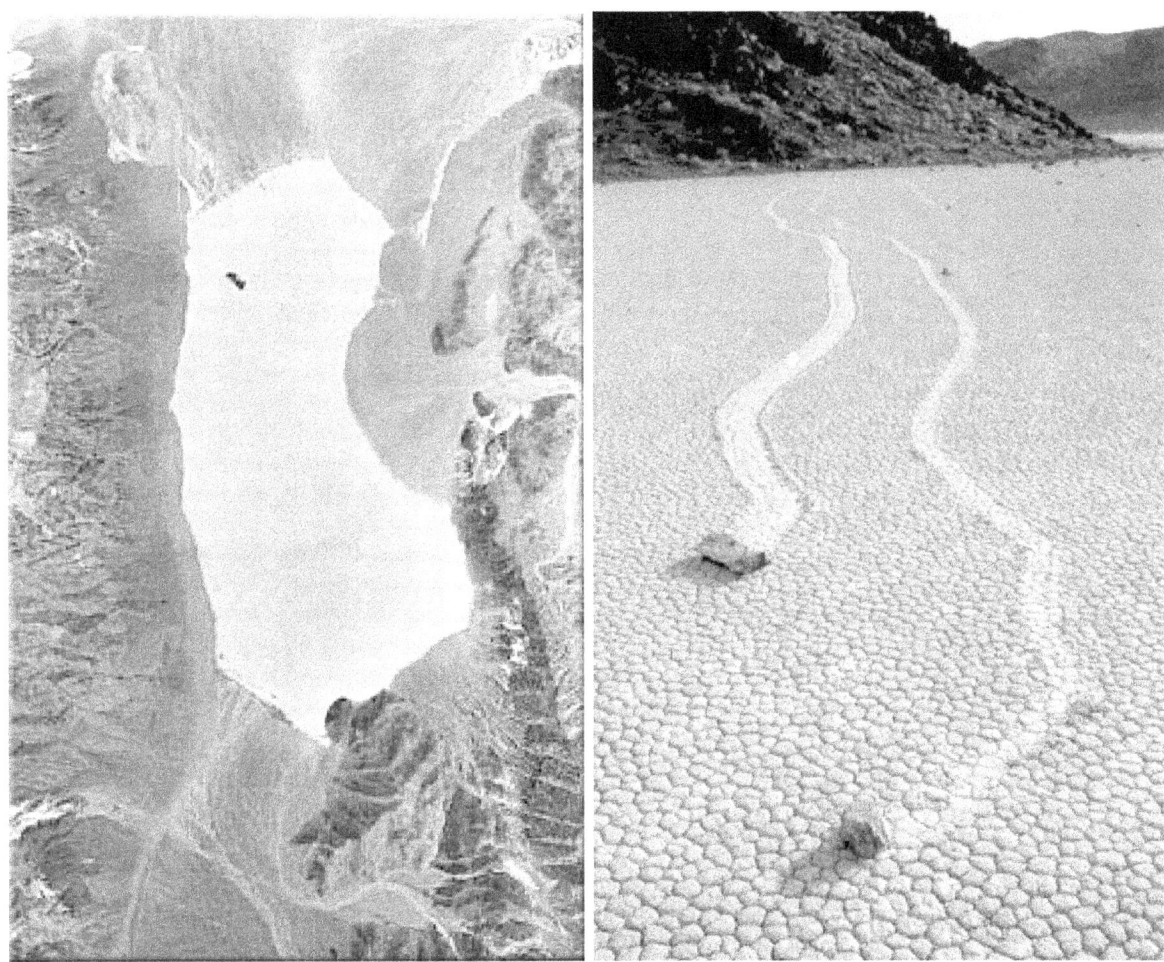

Ariel View of the Racetrack Playa; Photo: usgs.gov Moving Rocks; Photo: U.S. National Park Service

Sailing Rock Makes a Sudden Turn; Photo: Jon Sullivan

Moving Rock that's sliding across the desert on a corner; Photo: Jon Sullivan

Trails associated with these rocks suggest they came back to dock on the shore along the south end of the playa where they probably originated. Photo: usgs.gov

"Karen," a block of Racetrack Dolomite (named by Robert Sharp, 1976) is one of the largest of the sliding rocks on the Racetrack Playa. It is estimated to weigh between 700 and 800 pounds. Photo: usgs.gov

"Jesus Christ It's A Bigfoot!"
by Timothy Green Beckley

All Bigfoot photos this chapter by Joe Rauh

I think if I had seen him lumbering across the road I would have driven into a sandy ditch.

I mean, the last thing you would except to bump into in the middle of the desert – day OR night -- would be a *bona fide* Bigfoot. Sure up around Mount Shasta, the town of Weed or several settlements near the Oregon border, a big, tall, hairy creature wandering about with a mane down its back, might not shock the hell out of you like it would someone driving across the Mohave. One witness told me he was petrified, glued to the seat behind the steering wheel of the family camper, when he almost ran over this huge half-man, half-monster. "Jesus Christ it's a Bigfoot," he proclaimed to his wife and kids, as if they would have missed the creature so many have sighted all over the country, but is not normally thought of as making the desert its home.

When I was still a teenager I took a road trip several times to meet the man who had just about single handedly made the term Bigfoot internationally recognized. Ivan T. Sanderson was a prolific writer, a crypto zoologist with an MA in Botany, and Geology from Cambridge University. He had file cabinets full of authentic reports of sightings and close encounters but I doubt if he knew about the Bigfoot of the desert.

And to make matters worse, several of the sightings of Bigfoot were associated with the appearance of another controversial resident of the netherworld. In the November 1976 edition of Saga magazine, Peter Gutilla revealed how a group of witnesses camping in the northern Mojave Desert had watched as a torpedo-shaped object hovered over a ranch only to beam down three objects which "ambled" off in different directions. The witnesses said the "objects" were "animate" and one described two lights in what would approximate the area of the head (or two luminous eyes) of a reddish color. According to their testimony, the next day tracks were found in the area which couldn't be identified. Later, a convoy of military trucks appeared at the ranch and under the glare of spotlights, military personnel presumably "corralled" the Bigfoot and carted him off in a truck.

(Source: HighDesertBigfoot.com)

Douglas E. Trapp began collecting reports of the Desert Bigfoot back in the 70s. He's collected dozens of reports and feels that the creature is real and not a hoax (though some accounts may be). He says that in general they are very tall – 10 to 12 feet high – covered with short dark hair (as opposed to some of the reports he have received from the southern part of the state) and with feet that are freakishly large. Often they are curious about people and are known to pay particular attention to cars, trucks, trains and road signs. They can be aggressive and show no signs of fear as far as humans go. They only come out at night and walk along pavement to hide their tracks. They often have a terrible smell about them, and can be seen wandering around in small groups. The desert towns of Twenty Nine Palms, Joshua Tree, Indio and Anza-Borrego Desert State Park, are among the sites Trapp lists as far as believable sightings go.

MILITARY TRACKS BIGFOOT

The astute Mr. Trapp with his many years of research, notes the abundance of Bigfoot activity around the Mojave's Edwards Air Force Base, just north of Lancaster. Trapp says he had heard various rumors about sightings of a desert Bigfoot lurking about, but mum was the word.

That is, until finally several witnesses fessed up.

While scanning the perimeter through night vision field glasses a figure "very tall, hair-covered, ape-like" was spotted wandering the desert. Trapp says that the figure appeared to be searching aimlessly for something. Eventually, a helicopter appeared on the horizon and "spooked" the creature but good.

Eventually the desert Bigfoot were caught on sophisticated surveillance cameras but the tapes were never released because they were considered of a "high security" nature.

A major explained to the researcher that it was thought the beings were holding up in an underground tunnel system that runs under and around Edwards in the desert.

The appearance of the Bigfoot became almost a standing "joke" and a source of "entertainment." Some at the base connected the nocturnal sightings to UFOs that were also frequent visitors to the instillation and which had followed the space shuttle while landing on Edward's extra long landing strip.

Ann Slate and Allan Berry verified additional sightings made in the Golden State. The witnesses included police officers and more military personnel.

- Three Marines were frightened by an eight-foot, hair-covered "monster" that leaped in front of their car on the outskirts of Lancaster.
- Weeks later, an unkempt "man-thing" frightened some school kids who dubbed it the "Ragman of Palmdale."
- A Bakersfield newscaster was haunted by "inhuman screams" as he steered his Baja Buggy frantically through the night.
- Two youngsters saw a "huge thing" standing atop Lovejoy Butte.

And according to an article in the Yeti Researcher newsletter, Bigfoot was seen lurking behind Joshua trees, climbing fences and cruising campgrounds.

THE ROADSIDE MONSTER – TO BIG TO UGLY TO MISS!

The sightings throughout the desert have become so common, that Joe Rauh decided to fight fire with fire – or Bigfoot with Bigfoot I guess you might say.

As you drive past Joe's roadside workshop you can't miss the huge albino desert dwelling Bigfoot standing in front of his property. Why is it there you might ask? Rauh has a rational – seemingly! – explanation:

He attributes his roadside eye grabber to the various stories he has heard about the creature being seen in the vicinity. Rauh admits to being a "closet Bigfoot follower," having his ears pinned to the local entertainment channels for the latest sightings.

His intention was to create something that would catch a motorist's eye as he or she drove along standing out at 200 to 300 yards. He came up with a monster that is half Harry and the Henderson and the Patterson Bigfoot.

"These guys I have heard about are a little over 11 feet tall, probably about 250 lbs (still need to weight one)." Joe will make a Bigfoot to order. He sees it as something that is meant to arouse curiosity as well as make you stop and look around. Several of his monstrous figures are currently standing throughout the state to lure tourists into a strip mall or roadside diner.

Hopefully, these same tourists won't be confused between a real sighting of the desert Bigfoot and one of Joe's creations. There are various sites on the web to check out the real from the fantastic and if you want to see how Joe Rauh builds a monster from scratch just stroll on over to www.RoadsideMonster.com for all the lurid details. It's the next best thing to being confronted by a real life desert Bigfoot. . . we can guarantee you that!

Life After Death In Death Valley
by Timothy Green Beckley

I once spent Xmas in Death Valley with my friends Jackie and her sister Cindy. There was a fully dressed Yule tree in the bar area of the Furnace Creek Inn and I remember that the sunset was beyond description and a cool breeze added to the delightfulness of the evening. We chatted about ole times and about our drive through the desert along some of the most breathtaking settings the human eye could ever gaze upon

Before hitting the Inn for a seasonal glass of wine and a delicious meal, we had pulled off the road into the driveway of Scotty's Castle, where we would have liked to have taken the tour, but it was dark already and there were some very menacing predators lurking about whom we would have to deal with should we continue on foot unescorted. Yes indeed, the extremely aggressive wild ducks chased us about the parking lot, seemingly having been placed there to guard the perimeter of what is now a Death Valley landmark. And no doubt the ghost of Walter Scott needed all the protection he could garner, as his reputation as a charlatan who tried to con innocent investors into buying into his worthless gold mine eventually caught up to him. He had apparently invested not in gold mines but in himself, constructing a castle in "no mans land" that would be forever fit for a king.

Back at the Inn, as I recall we were very spirited in both our conversation and in our drinking habits. The subject of UFOs and aliens was a common bond between the three of us and as we went about our holiday cheeriness little did we know we might have had a true specter within our midst.

For the Furnace Creek Inn has a reputation for being haunted (say boo Ollie) . But be forewarned, there are no ghosts in white sheets as this nocturnal spirit is purported to be a friendly sort, and it's a wonder we didn't get to meet him as James Marquez is the former chef who had to take leave early due to a severe illness, dying within a year of his unscheduled retirement.

Chef Marquez is said to be the ultimate culinary ghost for he still likes to feel he is in control of the kitchen, putting things back in the places he best preferred for them, leaving open the refrigerator, as well as dumping out spices he doesn't favor. He can also be heard groaning from time to time to make his true feelings known. But if you listen to the skeptics and those who lack any psychic ability, they might just convince you it's nothing more goulash than the spirit of Death Valley calling from out of the night.

FIGARO, FIGARO, FIGARO

I thought Jackie was yanking my chain when she asked if I wanted to stop by the local opera house to see if Marta was going to be giving one of her famous operatic performances that evening.

Marta doesn't have to worry about a full house --
she has a built in (or should we say painted in?) audience.

After all what would an opera house be doing anywhere near Death Valley? And who was this semi-mysterious person known as Martha whose audience might be only a couple of tumble weeds?

I quickly learned that the Amargosa Hotel and Opera House gets more than its share of visitors and Marta was none other than Marta Beckley who was driving through Death Valley back in the late 1960's when her car broke down and she sought shelter in the old, dilapidated, opera house that had, in the Twenties, been the primary cultural hub for the Borax miners who lacked a movie theater or television in their day to entertain them during the desperately hot days and arid nights.

The Amargosa was one of Red Skelton's favorite places to be sequestered, Ray Bradbury would wander off to the hotel with his trusty typewriter to "lose himself" in thought for a few days, while most recently you might have caught Criss Angel performing a bit of magic amidst the haunted aisles.

If you buy a ticket and enter the opera house, don't expect to be serenaded by just any "Metropolitan Opera" diva, as the one and only performer is Marta Becket herself. Sure, there are stand-ins to be found dressed in flamboyant costumes – but they are only part of the many two-dimensional figures painted on the walls and ceilings as part of Marta's artistic expressionism. The numerous tapestries and murals add to the dreamlike quality of the opera house and hotel which seems to have stepped right out of time; only its fresh coat of whitewash on the outside cleverly disguises the fact that it's visitors have entered a proverbial time machine. For it's almost guaranteed that Marta Becket will not be the only one to entertain you, as a host of others long since deceased are sure to join in a passing parade of spirits.

Invisible hands may tap you on the shoulder as you sit in your seat, or a cool breeze may be felt as if someone is passing close by, quite noticeable considering the aridness of the setting. We understand there is even a little kitten that might pass between your toes while your eyes are upon the stage. Nevertheless, it's more likely upstairs along the corridors and in the hotel rooms that you will be approached by something truly supernatural. But you need not be afraid, as there are no accounts of anyone being given more than a good scare – a scare that will make you a believer forever that we never walk alone.

You need not take my word for it, however, for several ghost hunting groups toting the latest sensatory equipment can verify what I am saying. And they always have a credible psychic or sensitive amongst their ranks to add to the feedback from any preternatural specters attempting to show off from that place beyond the veil we call the afterlife.

It is within the the walls of the opera house that ghost hunters and visitors alike have felt the presence of a chilling cold spot in various locations throughout the structure.

It is along corridors upstairs in the hotel that ghost hunters have been confronted by phenomenon they cannot explain.

ENTER THE LOS ANGELES PARANORMAL ASSOCIATION

The Los Angeles Paranormal Association is a Los Angeles metro-area based group of investigators who came together with a common goal and interest. Their mission: "We seek to document physical evidence of the paranormal. To this end, we commonly investigate historical and/or reputably haunted locations and report on our findings."

The LAPA members found themselves in Death Valley on a special mission.

"We were there to see if spirits reside there now – and if so, who?" The group (Layla, Grant, Brian, Les, Kristen and Ty) maintain that they had received reports of a lot of unexplained phenomena at the Amargosa – "from phantom smells, to the sounds of babies crying to full bodied apparitions."

It was at night when the LAPA was being shown around by Marta herself. They were taken to some areas that are usually off limits to patrons of the arts.

"We visited a building at the rear of the property with a sad history – a young girl had drowned there. As we stood inside talking, several members of the group watched as a garden tool that was hanging from the wall started swinging with no visible cause. The wind was howling that night, but there were no major drafts in that room and the force of the swing was such that it would have taken more than a gust of wind to cause such a motion."

Inside the opera house itself they listened "as odd noises emanated from the walls," and, "watched as shadows outside moved across the opening at the bottom of the door."

Upstairs there is an abandoned, unrenovated section of the hotel affectionately referred to as "spooky hollow." We're told that this, "is the actual area where the miners stayed during the Pacific Borax days and includes what was the old hospital and morgue." The LAPA feel strongly that they have evidence that sections of "spooky hollow" have some unregistered guests staying there – including photos of strange orbs floating in midair.

The group plans to revisit the opera house to see if any other unexplainable phenomenon can be registered on their sophisticated ghost hunting equipment. Until then they remain convinced that the Amargosa "is a deeply fascinating and enigmatic place that touches the soul of those who pass through."

The full report filed by member "Layla Halfhill" can be found on
http://losangelesparanormalassociation.wordpress.com

Material On The Death Valley Opera House haunting courtesy - Layla Halfhill -Los Angeles Paranormal Association

Amargosa Opera House

Death Valley Junction, CA

Amargosa Hotel colonnade

hallway at Amargosa

Mysteries and Haunts of the Mojave Desert - Secrets of Death Valley

touring the property at night

spooky hollow hallway

spooky hollow - sun room

Marta during performance

Mural

room 19

Lobby Mural - Marta's Spirit and the Amargosa

The Hollywood Stars Are Big and Bright and So Are ALL the UFOs!
by Timothy Green Beckley

Let's be blunt, I'll never forget the scene with Peter Fonda and Jack Nicholson in Easy Rider as they hunker down around a camp fire in the California desert and begin to speak of all matters extraterrestrial.

"That was a UFO beamin' back at ya! Me and Eric Heisman was down in Mexico but 2 weeks ago and we'd seen 40 of 'em flying in formation. They...they...they've got bases all over the world now, you know. They've been coming here ever since 1946 when the scientists first started bouncing radar beams off of the moon. And they have been living and working among us in vast quantities ever since. The government knows all about 'em."

Just like our biker buddies in Easy Rider, the first thing you become aware of at night in the desert is the universe. It consumes you.

I mean the stars take on the appearance of radiant diamonds. I remember driving back to Palm Springs from the mouthwatering Hungarian restaurant Chef George located about twenty miles out into the desert, and being virtually speechless as the heavens encased me in their splendor. I tooled along in my convertible (the only way to experience the view) marveling about how much of the universe there is to see, normally invisible to those of us who have chosen to live in an urban environment.

Later on, after one of my UFO Expos held in Palm Springs, we set up a telescope by the pool and what I had seen with the naked eye had now increased two fold. It may not be this way anymore, because of all the shopping malls and fast food joints continually polluting the atmosphere with their klieg lights and dazzling neon, but the night sky in the desert was breathtaking in those days.

Being only a few hours drive from LA you would expect that a few celebrity types might wander through the desert from time to time stumbling upon something that will effect their lives, just like it does to those not fortunate enough to be walking around with a silver spoon in their mouths (or a press agent in tow).

I remember Shirley MacLaine talking about the Petroglyphs in the desert and how some of them showed what appeared to be saucer-shaped flying machines and commenting about how these Petroglyphs must pay homage to those who came out of the sky in their flying machine.

Further out on the cosmic trail, rock poet and musician Jim Morrison seems to have been caught up since an early age with the spirits of Native Americans. Morrison reports that he was driving across the desert with his family when they got involved in a tragic accident. A truck filled with Indians had crashed head on into another vehicle and there were bodies all over the blacktop. Situated in the back seat, at first the rock troubadour to be had no idea of what was going on up in front. He is quoted: ". . .all I saw was funny red paint and people lying around, but I knew something was happening, because I could dig the vibrations of the people around me, and all of a sudden I realized that they didn't know what was happening any more than I did. That was the first time I tasted fear. . .and I do think, at that moment, the souls of those dead Indians – maybe one or two of them – were just running around, freaking out, and just landed in my soul, and I was like a sponge, ready to sit there and absorb it."

Wow tripe.

In addition to being the Goddess of Libido, Mae West was also a psychic and a devoted spiritualist. The bombshell blonde did a lot of her table tipping and spirit rapping in the desert at the famed La Quinta Resort just out of Indio. It was here that she seemed to get her first taste of the world of spirits insisting that her father was able to speak with her even though he was not still among the living.

Emily Leider, author of Becoming Mae West, acknowledges West's fascination with the spiritual:

"Mae felt herself drawn back into the world of spiritualism, which promised contact with the dead. At a resort called La Quinta, which was frequented by Paramount executives, she met Amelia Earhart, who shared this mystical bent. Mae had long admired Earhart for her courage and her mastery of the sky, "a man's world"...and the two pioneers-one in aviation, the other in sexuality- talked about their mutual interest in psychic explorations.... After the séance with Amelia Earhart, Mae concentrated on developing her psychic powers. Each day she retreated to a dark room, where she sat, meditating, on a straight back chair, placing her hands on her knees."

Blame it on the desert – spiritualism stayed with her all of her life thanks to what happened in the Mojave.

SAMMY DAVIS JR AND THE RAT PACK

Sammy Davis Jr. and drummer Buddy Rich used to hang out in Vegas and swap UFO stories. Rich was a dear friend of the late astronomer Dr J. Allen Hynek who had once been with the Air Force's Project Blue Book and was nicknamed Professor Swamp Gas when he suggested, kind of off the cuff, that a rash of sightings near Ann Arbor, Michigan might have been caused by a natural will of the wisp discharge from marshy soil. Hynek later altered his skeptical beliefs to that of a believer in UFOs, and one wonders how much effect hanging out with the two Rat Pack members convinced him to go against his original thinking.

I spoke with both Davis and Rich and can confirm that they were more than just casually interested in flying saucers. Rich had a number of sightings detailed in my book UFOS Among The Stars, but none were in the California desert. Sammy Davis Jr. also came close to the unknown, but our interest here is in the following sighting because it took place in the area we were fascinated with. But we have to give Buddy a lot of credit, for he was the one who set up a phone conversation with Davis, so that we could speak to him as he hung out from his dressing room backstage at one of the finer casino's on the Vegas Strip.

"My most impressive sighting," says Davis, "was just outside of Palm Springs. There were a lot of sightings around 1952-53 and I wasn't to be left out."

Sammy says he was with a group when they spotted the discs as they literally "floated overhead." He was amazed at how they could accelerate from a dead stop to almost fantastic speeds. "First they would stand still and then they would take off and stop again, before finally shooting away in a flash."

MICHAEL BOATMAN AND A PARADIGM SHIFT

As co-star of the ABC comedy series Spin City, Michael Boatman hardly ever had the opportunity to show his serious side. But that's not to say that the author of God Laughs When You Die wasn't capable of being serious once in a while, just like the time he described how he had stopped to stretch by the side of the road in the Mojave on his way to Palm Springs. "High above my head I saw it; a luminous, circular object, reddish in color, hovering motionless way up in the clear blue California sky. I stared at the object for a while. It was a perfectly cloudless afternoon, and although I had no idea what I was seeing, I could see the thing hanging up there as clearly as I could see the public Men's room outside which I was loitering. Moments later, the object vanished from view. I don't know if it teleported or passed behind a cloud or made the jump into hyperspace; all I can say is that the shining red object was there one moment and gone the next. Despite my best efforts I couldn't find it again."

Boatman has obviously studied the subject for he makes mention of an upswing in "large-scale mass sightings of UFOs in the media, from a Mexico City flap which began during a lunar eclipse in the mid-nineties and continues to this day, to the Phoenix Lights mass-sighting over Arizona and Nevada ten years go."

So why is the government so worried about mass hysteria? Boatman explains it this way: "This kind of data always threatens people, particularly the very religious, but why? What actually makes us think we're so special? Simple ignorance? Arrogance? A belief in a human-friendly, anthropomorphic God/Genie who listens to our wishes and chooses which ones to answer based on adherence to a moral code created by ancient goat- herders? Do these people think that if ET shows up as a chlorophyll-based multi-gendered atheistic telepathic collective, say, or a cloud of sentient ammonia particles, that their own belief systems will crumble and fall by the wayside? Historically speaking, primitive cultures always collapse when confronted by a technically superior culture. Is this what the theocrats fear? The answer is a resounding 'Yes!'

"And I believe the death of such cultural bigotry can't happen quickly enough."

PLEASE MR SPACEMAN TAKE US FOR A RIDE

I've long had knowledge that strange things transpire in the Mojave. The late astronaut Gordon Cooper once called me to talk about UFOs. He had heard that I had mentioned him on a radio show and wanted to set the record straight and give me details about an incident involving him that I wasn't fully informed about.

He had been stationed at Edwards Air Force Base in the Mojave where he was a Project Manager. It was either 1957 or 58 and there had been sightings of UFOs near the base. A team of photographers were under Cooper's command and one day they excitedly entered his office. The men said they had seen an object in the sky which moments later landed. It was a typical disc-shaped craft resting on a tripod landing gear. The object rested on the dry lake bed of Edwards and then took off going straight up.

Cooper had the film developed and had it screened numerous times. Sure enough it was just like he had been told, convincing the astronaut that it was not a military drone or something built by a foreign power. To the day he died Cooper couldn't hazard a guess to the UFO's origin, though he was pretty much convinced it hadn't been manufactured on earth. Cooper's credibility adds substance to the many reports in the Mojave and so they can't be debunked so easily as they world if he hadn't been involved.

Canadian born actor and Star Trek stalwart William Shatner had his own UFO experience he wanted to relate, as we met back stage at the Ed Sullivan theater in NYC where he was taping a weeks worth of the Ten Thousand Dollar Pyramid hosted by Dick Clark.

"I'll tell you a story that happened to me, and is open to any kind of interpretation you wish.

"In the late '60s when Star Trek was on, there were a lot of UFOs being sighted in the desert near Palmdale, California. We heard all kinds of stories about these objects, crafts, spaceships – call them what you will. There was even one fellow who said he talked with creatures from space. During this period, I used to drive my motorcycle a great deal, and would occasionally head for the wide-open span of sand and sun. With my sense of humor, I'd say to myself, 'Well if I were a little green man in a flying saucer and wanted to get publicity' – which is what they would seem to be seeking –who would I contact faster than Captain Kirk of the Star Ship Enterprise? Often Shatner says he would wonder if they were capable of picking up the thoughts of earthlings.

"One day I was out driving with four other guys, around noon, that's the hottest part of the day in the desert, when I hit a hole and fell from my bike. I must have fainted when the bike collapsed on top of me. When I came to, I estimate that I was unconscious for only about a minute, I could get my motorcycle started. The motor refused to turn over. . . So ere I am in the middle of the desert with a metal helmet on, wearing a leather jacket, heavy pants, boots and a machine next to me worth close to five thousand dollars." Shatner didn't want to leave the bike behind but it was definitely too heavy to carry or to even push along. It was at this point that he happened to see something gleaming in the blistering sunlight.

"It was like when you have a nightmare and you feel something crawling over your body or wrestling with you. As you awaken from the dream it turns out your blanket was the thing crawling over you. In other words, it was more of a sensing – a feeling – a shadowy phantom. All I know, positively, is that I suddenly felt better.

"As I said, when I came to I couldn't get the bike to move. No matter what I did it refused to start. Finally, I tried pushing it up a hill, but it wouldn't go in that direction. Then I turned around and decided to go down the hill, but it still wouldn't budge. Nor did it obey my command to turn left. Eventually, I shoved it to the right and it began to move as though it was going some place on its own. But this time I was doing what I was feeling. One could say I was doing what I was told to, but I was just doing the easiest possible thing.

"Fantastic as it may, seem, the motorcycle appeared to have a way of going on its own. At this point I thought I saw somebody – another cyclist – in the distance waving me on, and so I continued to struggle with the heavy metal monster until I stumble upon civilization in the form of a gas station in the middle of the desert, resting at the side of an old paved road."

Some critics may say that Shatner created this account for the sake of publicity. Did his potentially life saving UFO experience really happen, or can we put it down as an urban legend of the Mojave told by one of the most entertaining actors of our time? I guess you need to draw your own conclusion. In the meanwhile, you can beam me up Scotty!

Movie poster takes Death Valley name a bit too far –
certainly not to be endorsed by the local Chamber of Commerce.

Mysteries and Haunts of the Mojave Desert - Secrets of Death Valley

The Skidoo Mining District was one of the last gold mining efforts in Death Valley. Gold deposits were discovered in 1906. The town of 23 Skidoo grew to almost 500 people by the following year. Production of gold ore continued intermittently until the rich gold veins played out in 1917. Today the town of 23 Skidoo consists only of a few ruins. The ruins of the mine's ore processing works are shown here. 23 Skidoo, or just Skidoo, probably got its name from the usage of the phrase of "23 Skidoo" by police in New York City who used to say "23 Skidoo" when chasing women-watching Bowery bums away from the Flatiron Building (once the tallest building in Manhattan at the intersections of 23rd Street, Broadway, and 5th Avenue). Photo: usgs.gov

The Furnace Creek Museum has an outdoor historic wagon exhibit that includes everything from stagecoaches to borax ore carts. Photo: usgs.gov

There Is Still Gold In Them There Dunes

So you think the gold rush is over?

That you won't get rich turning the sand and soil looking for gold nuggets just like they did back when prospectors fought with their lives to hold onto their claim?

Truth be truth -- it is said that only one percent of all the gold has been extracted from the Mojave Desert. That means you could spend years and years just digging around for what could make you a very wealthy person. Of course, you'll need a grub stake, some fairly heavy – and expensive – equipment as well as a team of loyal workers who won't turn against you or stab you in the back (literally!).

Mojave Desert, Here We Come! Miners, Homesteaders, and Route 66

During the mid-19th century, mining in all areas of the Mojave created boom towns with colorful names and characters. On Christmas Day in 1860, for example, the first producing Mojave mine, named "Christmas Gift," was opened in Death Valley. As the mining boom continued, borax—"the white gold of the desert"—was discovered; it has been mined profitably in the Death Valley area since. During the 1870s, the Clark Mountain Mining district was established and with it the town of Ivanpah, which at the time was the only American community of any size in the eastern portion of the Mojave.

Gold was discovered in El Dorado Canyon in the late 19th century, where a single mine ultimately produced $1.7 million in gold. Small prospectors, however, generally made very little money, the biggest problem being the costs of transporting supplies to such remote locations. "Boom-or-bust" mining was the usual approach: As soon as a strike played out, miners moved on, leaving ghost towns in their wake.

With the coming of the Santa Fe Railroad, water and other supplies were made available to companies intent on capitalizing on the Mojave's resources. In the early 1900s, more mines were open and profitable in the Mojave than at any previous time, establishing such towns as Cima,

Kelso, and Fenner. Demand for Mojave metals such as gold, silver, and manganese, peaked during World Wars I and II.

Today most Mojave mining is for gold and nonmetals such as borax. Beginning in 1910, land was homesteaded in the Mojave Desert, usually in 64.8 ha (160 ac) parcels. Claimants had three years in which to improve their properties to receive a deed from the General Land Office, a predecessor of the Bureau of Land Management. Among the came from other parts of California to settle in the Lanfair Valley area.

Developed in California's Ivanpah Valley in the mid-1980s as a small, open-pit, heap-leach operation, the now-abandoned Morningstar Gold Mine has the potential to cause cyanide-related environmental problems.
U.S. GEOLOGICAL SURVEY

For a few years after 1912, rainfall was relatively plentiful, and crop production was vigorous enough that more people were attracted to the area. Mustard-gas victims of World War I also came to take advantage of the benefits of the dry desert air. Ultimately, the rains didn't last, and water rights conflicts erupted between homesteaders and ranchers. In many cases, after digging unsuccessful water wells, homesteaders were forced to haul water for several kilometers for household use. Many small farms and homesteads were abandoned with only tiny cabins left behind.

A Mojave Desert homesteader poses at California's Lanfair Valley railroad station, which was served by the Nevada Southern Railway. A branch railroad of the Atchison, Topeka, and the Santa Fe Railway until it closed in 1923, the Nevada Southern line was the main economic lifeline of the high country in the eastern Mojave.
COURTESY OF MOJAVE DESERT ARCHIVES

During the 1920s, Route 66 appeared out of a desire to improve the road network in the West, which featured a hodgepodge of tracks and trails that had been established by American Indians and pioneers. A descendant of the early 1900s "National Old Trails Road," the new two-lane route would join the Midwest to California. Route 66 was also to become a legend—"the Mother Road" and "the Main Street of America"—immortalized in John Steinbeck's The Grapes of Wrath, Nat King Cole's "(Get Your Kicks on) Route 66," and a popular 1960s television show. During the Great

Depression of the 1930s migrants sought out the Mojave as an area where they might be able to grow their own food without regard for unstable world markets. Sandstorms and drought drove millions from the Dust Bowl toward California on Route 66. During and after World War II Americans traveled the route heavily, though the roadway was narrow and accidents frequent. In 1956 interstate highways, including Routes 40, 15, and 10 through Arizona and California, began to skirt around the towns along Route 66 closely paralleling the older route. By 1985 the last of these, Williams, Arizona, was bypassed.

It is no longer necessary to drive any part of Route 66 to reach California from Chicago. However, a new generation of travelers has made a hobby of tracing authentic pieces of the highway, following the "Historic Route 66" signs that began appearing in 1995 in all of the route's eight states.

As Historic Route 66 meanders through the Black Mountains of western Arizona, it presents travelers with hairpin curves and steep grades—some of the most fearsome obstacles along its length.
GORDON WARREN, BLM

Some text courtesy U.S. Bureau Of Land Management

It may be a "lost mine" to some, but this looks like a big enough marker to point anyone in the right direction. (Courtesy Kokoweef Corporation)

The "Lost" Kokoweef Cavern and Money Pit Now "Found"

Earlier in these pages, we discussed the mysterious caverns found by Earl P. Dorr. Many believe that the entrance to this vast system and its potentially immense assets are a closely guarded secret having long been swallowed up by time and her partner mother earth.

The truth is a bit more complex than that .

William Halliday, in his book Adventure Is Underground, asks the very important question:

"Is this just an imaginary cave?" No, the cave certainly exists. There are those who have seen it! "Did Dorr keep it's location secret?' No. Dozens, perhaps hundreds, of people know it's exact location, high on the side of Kokoweef Peak in the Mojave Desert. "

Has anyone tried to find this river of gold?' Yes, indeed! The Kokoweef Mining Corporation owns the property where the gold is too be found. . . or so they say.

If this all seems farfetched and difficult believe ... IT CERTAINLY IS!

But it's all wrapped up as part and parcel of the lore and urban legends of the desert. Many who keep to the byways and dusty trails (as well as to themselves), pass on such claims. Thus in the by-and-by, truth becomes mingled with hearsay making for a good ole tall tale. There are those "in the know" who have started their own mining company and who equally maintain that the gold is available for the "taking" and investors are not frowned upon. If interested in gold mining and what must be considered a highly calculated risk, mossy on over to the following internet site www.kokoweef.com and find out what this is all about. . .as this is from where we obtained the various photos and where you can see many more for yourself.

LOST MINES OF THE OLD WEST

The Golden Cavern of Kokoweef Mountain

Think of it! "Eight miles of gold-bearing black sand for an average width of three hundred and fifty feet and an average depth of eight feet along the banks of a river." That is the sworn statement of the finder of this legendary mine. And the river of the golden sands is in a great cavern two thousand feet underground!

The discoverer's affidavit also tells of an assay of the sand by a prominent chemist of Los Angeles showing the gold value of $2,145.47 a cubic yard at the old gold price of $20.67 an ounce. But sit tight while you read this story. Don't pack the old kit bag for a mad rush to this bonanza. It is in the hands of a syndicate and no shares are for sale. Nor will this once-lost mine be lost again.

At the time of this writing no one can say that the tale is true in actual detail, but reasons exist for suspecting that it has at least some foundation in fact. And operations are under way to learn the truth. If even a small part of this fantastic yarn is verified it would seem to belie conviction of the tired wage-earner that the last chapter of gold, of new unseen gold, has been written in musty books, and to deny his plaint that days of opportunity are over. And this story of how an Indian legend came to life will have its value, for the yarn is more far-fetched than the wildest of lost mine stories cooked up by a campfire. And those who are ready to laugh off all legends of lost lodes and vanished placer beds may think again of the great cavern beneath the floor of the desert.

Imagine finding this stream of cool water flowing over its golden sands down in vast, dark depths of a secret cavern—yes, beneath the Mojave Desert, where many a thirst-crazed gold-seeker has left his bones to bleach under the merciless sun! Imagine it, a scarce sixty miles south of the searing bottom of Death Valley! Imagine finding it almost alongside the concrete ribbon of U. S. Highway 91 (and 466) only sixty-five miles from Las Vegas. The artisans of Boulder Dam, twenty minutes away by air, would not have dreamed of it. Remember, too, the old days of the Spanish Trail, a few miles away, beaten again by the feet of Fremont and his men in 1844, and the Garces route of 1776, not twenty miles to the south, followed again in 1827 by Jedediah Smith and his crew. And give a thought then to the real pioneers of the desert's mineral wealth—those grim, lone, slouch-hatted men of pick and pan and patient burro—the misty horde of prospectors who passed this way through the long years and vanished into the sunset.

Perhaps no one will ever know just how long the cavern of the Ivanpah Mountains, near the eastern border of California, and of Kokoweef Peak, in particular, was known to the Indians. However, its known history begins years ago when the man whose affidavit, given below, was a small boy. Two Indians known to him and his father on their Colorado ranch gave the boy a map to hidden treasure, so they said, telling him that when he grew up he could get rich. Coming as it did, this news was given no more credulity than one might expect. An Indian legend that might have something in it, some time. The boy, now known as E. P. Dorr, kept the map, "grew up" and followed its directions. There was something in it. Dorr claims that the story told by the Indians appeared to be true.

Originally there had been three Indians, brothers, and from tribal history they had found again the small entrance to a cave so vast that no one could know its extent. Far down inside, down, down, was a river of rushing water. Along the banks was much gold, the Indians said. It was mixed with the black sands so no one could say how much was there. The three brothers had sifted and carried away much placer gold, but the tragedy of the yellow metal finally reached down into the cave and struck. Once while carrying their primitive torchlights, one brother fell down over a great cliff in the darkness and his brains were dashed out on the rocks below. According to tribal tradition, the two remaining brothers were forever barred from returning to the scene of the death, hence their gift of the map and its story to young Dorr.

Dorr's story is told in the following statement, sworn in an affidavit on November 16, 1934, and published in the *California Mining Journal* of November, 1940. The statement is reprinted through the courtesy of that publication.

DORR'S AFFIDAVIT

"This is to certify that there are located in San Bernardino County, California, certain caverns. These caverns are about 250 miles from Los Angeles, California. Traveling over state highways by automobile the caverns can be reached in a few hours.

"Accompanied by a mining engineer, I visited the caverns in the month of May, 1927. We entered them and spent four days exploring them for a distance of between eight and nine miles. We carried with us altimeters and pedometers to measure the distance we traveled and had an instrument to take measurements of distance by triangulation, together with such instruments . . . to make examinations, observations and estimations.

"Our examinations revealed the following facts:

"1. From the mouth of the cavern we descended about 2,000 feet. There we found a canyon which, on our altimeter, measured about 3,000 to 3,500 feet deep. We found the caverns to be divided into many chambers, filled and embellished with the usual stalagmites and stalactites, besides many grotesque and fantastic wonders that make the caverns one of the marvels of the world.

"2. On the floor of the canyon there is a flowing river which . . . we estimated to be about 300 feet wide and with considerable depth. The river rises and falls with the tides of the sea, at high tide being about 300 feet wide and at low tide about 10 feet wide and 4 feet deep.

"3. When the tide is out there is exposed on both sides of the river from 100 to 150 feet of black beach sand which is very rich in gold values. The sands are from 4 to 11 feet deep. This means there are about 300 to 350 feet of rich bearing placer sand which average 8 feet in depth. We explored the canyon sands a distance of more than 8 miles, finding little variation in the depth and width of the sands.

"4. I am a practical miner of many years experience and I own valuable mining properties nearby which I am willing to pledge and put up as security to guarantee that the statements herein made are true.

"5. My purpose of exploring the caverns was to study the mineralogy in order to ascertain the mineral possibilities and actualities of the caves, making such examination in person with my engineer to determine by expert examination the character and quantity of mineral values.

"6. I carried out about 10 pounds of the black sand and 'panned it,' receiving more than $7.00 in gold. I sold it to a gold buyer who allowed me at the rate of $18.00 per ounce. Two and one-half pounds of this black sand I sent to John Herman, assayer, whose assay certificates show a value of $2,145.47 per yard, with gold at $20.67 per ounce.

"7. From engineering measurements and observations we made I estimated that it would require a tunnel about 350 feet long to penetrate to the caverns, one thousand feet or more below the present entrance, which is some three miles distant from my property.

"8. I make no estimate of even the approximate tonnage of the black sand, but some estimate of the cubical contents may be made for more than eight miles and the minimum depth is never less than three feet. They are of varying depth—what their maximum depth may be we do not know."

Needless to say, publication of the above affidavit caused a flurry in mining circles at the time, but nothing came of it. Obviously any development of such a property called for extensive resources. Dorr's story changed in minor details from that told in the affidavit but still stretches credulity. The two men told of climbing 1,200 feet down from the opening on top of Kokoweef Mountain between overlaying limestone and metamorphic rock beneath it. The cavern below was of unknown size and the small stream, after a few miles, finally plunged over a precipice 3,000 feet high, or that much farther down into the earth!

Dorr and his partner filled pockets with specimens of sand, but the steep climb was too much for the partner, so Dorr had to assist him and was reviving the man when other prospectors appeared. Some of the sand was spilled and likewise the secret. Dorr climbed down and set off dynamite charges at two points to seal the cave, the upper one 300 feet below the opening. That level is as far as anyone has been able to descend and the engineers decided against reopening the natural entrance. Instead they have started to drill at a lower level for the sake of a shorter shaft. At the time of this writing no one has peered into the strange depths below.

Meanwhile the traditional fatality of gold has struck once more. Dorr's partner died, from natural causes. And Dorr is out of the picture. The two men spoke of rushing winds in the cave. They believed that the draught could exist only because of a second opening which they imagined they saw, far away in the roof, apparently offering easier access. Both were so convinced of this that they allowed their registered claim to the original entrance to go by default. Another prospector then staked the claim and sold it. Meanwhile Dorr has failed to find a clue leading to another entrance.

Fantastic as this story sounds, both Dorr and his partner have told it separately to persons unknown to each other and in substantially the same version. Inquiry has disclosed that even the Indian brothers of the tale had bank accounts of proportions. And a desert river out there does disappear from the surface. The mining firm in control at the time this is written is already operating a producing zinc mine on the same mountain, almost right at the spot. In a talk with a member of this company, he told the writer—"we don't know what we will find. We just discount the whole thing one hundred per cent and then we know we at least will have a lot of fun."

Discussing the Aladdin Cave angles of what is a venture into matter-of-fact hard rock with an outlay of modern cash, the writer said: "When you get the gold out, just let me have the tourist rights." For if there is a 3,000-foot waterfall under Kokoweef Mountain, then an

Is it possible that a vast treasure rests beneath this spot in the desert of California? (Courtesy Kokoweef Corporation)

intriguing bit of scenery would seem to have escaped from Yosemite Valley and hid underground. Yet, the geologists who have walked over the terrain say there can be little doubt of the existence of a giant cavern down there—how big is only a guess. Could it be another Carlsbad? They are definitely interested.

If a half of the Arabian Nights elements of this sworn tale materialize, the most modern of realists will concede a bit of sympathy for the lure that drew the swashbuckling conquistadores over endless reaches of desert and dale in search of the Seven Cities of Cibola.

It is beneath this hollowed ground that the Kokoweef "money pit" is said to exist. (Courtesy Kokoweef Corporation)

Happy Trails
by Timothy Green Beckley

Let's be blunt, I'll never forget the scene with Peter Fonda and Jack Nickelson in *Easy Rider* as they hunker down around a crackling camp fire and begin to speak of things extraterrestrial. "That was a UFO beamin' back at ya! Me and Eric Heisman was down in Mexico about two weeks ago and we'd seen 40 of 'em flying in formation. They...they...they've got bases all over the world now, you know. They've been coming here ever since 1946 when the scientists first started bouncing radar beams off of the moon. And they have been living and working among us in vast quantities ever since. The government knows all about 'em'"

On the other hand, I'm the kind of person who likes to coast into a nice motel or resort and partake of the grandeur the way God and my American Express card intended. Its easy to spend a bundle being a paranormalist in the desert in search of some of the strangest and most peculiar sites and experiences you are likely ever too partake of. It is awful tempting to say the hell with it and set up base camp in Palm Springs and do day trips from there. But if you're serious and want to really get down with nature and hob knob with the unseen its possible to be brave and tempt the elements.

Roadside adventurer Al Fry is a man of the world – well maybe many worlds. During the 1970's he created some of the most outrageous documentaries on video. They might have been crudely produced by today's standards, but the information provided was one of a kind. Subjects like time travel and alien hybrids. Weird stuff. Not the kind of videos the big studios would go near. Al traveled through the byways and out of the way highways of the desert, and unlike yours truly, made his home at the side of the road not caring to spend the "big bucks" that have made the credit card companies filthy rich. "During the last ten years I have spent less than a dozen dollars a week on an average for direct living expenses," he explains. No SUV to fill up with petrol, All was content to settle upon various stages of step-in vans, but finally settled upon a van with the whole works, paneling and all. What kind of van? A reconditioned, purchased at auction, bread truck that he pulled a little French Citroen behind that gave him the opportunity to veer off and do some sightseeing.

Fry says he camped with permission "gypsy style" near some of California's most interesting areas. But he always loved the desert most of all because, "The desert is full of beautiful places, and surprises. An old favorite of mine when coming or going is Whitewater River Canyon, about 10 miles north of Palm Springs, just off Indio Freeway. The river runs the year around there and the only hang up is occasional wind." Though we've never communicated about it specifically, I've seen it posted that Mr. Fry got interested in many of the fringe subjects promoted in his video series (type in his name on YouTube) by attending a couple of George Van tassel's conventions out at Giant Rock. Though retired today in Idaho, he is well thought of and remembered by those who have made the desert their home.

VISIONS IN THE DESERT

Earlier we described the visionary experiences of Dana Howard who witnessed the materialization of a space woman while accompanied by more than two dozen eyewitnesses. There is no end to the prophetic new agers who populated the desert landscape in decades past with their talk of benevolent space gods who arrived on earth to share their wishes for a more peaceful earth community so that we could join our brethren as a member of the intergalactic federation of planets. Fanciful stuff hey?

Among the UFO contactees no one was more beloved than Orfeo Angelucci whose experiences seemed partly physical, and partly psychic in nature. It was while Orfeo was driving home from work that he began experiencing a tingling sensation. A luminous disc appeared ahead of him as if on a screen. Beings from another world escorted him aboard and gave him a goblet and he drank from it and relieved his unpleasant sensation. After a short conversation the beings promised to return and disappeared. Some saw Orefo's and other such metaphysical accounts to be pure fantasy, while others became reverent supporters of the cosmic peacenik movement. But so much for UFOlogical matters for the moment. What of those individuals who are a bit less cosmic in their spirituality? For certainly the desert belongs to all of us regardless of our religious orientation.

On the 13th of each month upwards of a thousand devotees gather in the desert outside of California City waiting for an apparition of the

Virgin Mary. Known as Our Lady of the Rock, believers say they can smell the scene of roses when Mary is nearby and that it is not uncommon for rose peddles to fall from the sky. While only Maria Paula Acuna, a 45-year-old Catholic can communicate with her, cameras continually click away aimed primarily toward the sky in hopes of picking up some unusual phenomenon through their view finder. Prints of photos are passed around showing mysterious bands and pulsations of light, orbs, translucent figures and various other abnormalities.

Surrounded by her inner circle dressed entirely in white robes, Mrs. Acuna says the apparition looks no more than 18 years old and usually comes in the form of a cloud and materializes – except on rare occasions -- only to her. Some miraculous healings have been reported though this is certainly not the grotto at Lourdes. In fact, the Church has frowned on the visions and has suggested that the apparitions are a matter of wishful fantasizing. But you can't tell the multitude anything of this sort, as they gather in clusters and parade across the desert holding larger than life crosses in homage to the mother of Jesus.

ORBS, ORBS, AND EVEN MORE ORBS

Musician John Pederson believes so strongly in what he saw – what frightened him half to death on a night in May, 1997, in the area of Anza-Borrego State Park – that he has devoted almost an entire blog to the orbs that seem to be intent on "attacking" him. Though some think that Pederson is using this as an opportunity to promote his most recent album Legend and Landscape, for all intense and purposes he seems incredibly sincere while revealing details of his experience.

The artist, who has won many awards, says he was planning a nighttime hike in order to avoid the heat of the day. Pederson had traveled two hours from San Diego before parking and walking into the desert under his own steam. The light from the moon acted as a beacon enabling him to traverse the area without twisting an ankle or falling down. It was breezy, but still fairly warm. When he reached an area where there was an old dolomite mine and some dilapidated machinery, John noticed something peculiar about 50 yards up ahead that was flicking on the side of a hill.

Pederson's first thought that someone had set up a camp site and started a fire to keep away unwelcome animals as well as a chill that was bound to come up later in the night. It was just after 10 AM that he found himself under siege. . . and we're not talking snakes and coyotes here. Let John explain:

"After several minutes, I noticed a faint, ethereal ball of light around the size of a baseball coming down slowly from the top of the hill (around 100 feet up). Inside the ball was a gentle white to bluish phosphorescent light that flickered randomly. When the first orb was around halfway down the hill, a second one emerged from the top. After another 5 minutes, a third orb was slowly moving down from the top with the first orb now at the bottom of the hill 50 yards away. At this point in time, being very, very spooked, I turned around and decided to head back to the car. Walking toward the South, I saw two lights approaching with no sound. However, as those lights passed overhead, I heard the sound of jet engines on a fighter. The F14 or F18 flew right over the top of my location at only about 300-500 feet overhead. There is an Air Force base 20 miles to the east in El Centro and on the other side of the hillside where the glowing orbs were, is the abandoned Carrizo Impact Zone. This is a 'closed' practice bombing area that hasn't been used in years because of a large number of unexploded ordinances in that area. Fighter jets do fly very low to the ground in the desert because there are no altitude restrictions, but having one fly right over me (with the orbs) was very strange. My first thought was that something weird was perhaps going on in the Impact Zone just over the hill. However, at this point in time, I wasn't interested in finding out what. Now worked up into a state of panic, I ran the 2 miles back to the car without looking back."

John says he returned to the exact spot on another day with his girlfriend to see if they could find any evidence lying around. Though they didn't hear or see anything weird, John says his lady became overcome with a feeling of dread. He dually notes he is not alone in his encounter with these orbs. "This area has a long tradition of 'balls of light' flying through the air, all kinds of ghost stories and all manner of unusual events. My 2nd album, Legend And Landscape, was inspired by these stories."

Just a couple of months later, researcher Bill Hamilton reveals that a, "series of visitors reported seeing in the early evening hours, white-and-orange orbs hovering in the sky southeast of El Mirage." The author of Cosmic Top Secret says that "the orbs seemed to hover for long periods of time before zipping away at unimaginable speeds. Minutes later the sight would appear again and repeat the maneuver. One evening in

April 1998, to the north in Rosamond, residents shopping and eating diner were awed by a large hovering object sighted above the Albertson's supermarket off 15th Street West and Rosamond Boulevard." The sightings were near the Gray Butte military facility and witnesses who wandered into the desert saw what they described as bright white and orange orbs. There are those who believe the objects might be part of secret tests of a classified anti-gravity device which is fifty years ahead of anything we have in the sky – that is known about – today. Hamilton repeats stories about how the craft are housed underground and are lifted to the surface through huge doors that open and close making it hard for them to be detected.

BRING IN THE CLOWNS

Oh travelers of the open road beware of a 12 foot clown striding along as the time approaches Midnight. It may just be a case of Coulrophobia -- or it would be a secret government experiment taking place near Death Valley.

I have a dear friend who is so deadly scared senseless of clowns, that she can never go to a circus with her children or even a rodeo where clowns jump in and out of barrels and hoops in order to protect the rodeo riders from some of the biggest, meanest, bulls on earth. There have even been a couple of articles written on the subject of how clown paranoia is so wide spread. The phobia even has its own name -- Coulrophobia.

As a bit of background, John – *Mothman Prophecies* -- Keel wrote about how some UFO witnesses were being harassed in Point Pleasant, WV by clowns who would come to the front door of those who had witnessed the creature or seen a UFO at close range, to ask meaningless questions or to threaten them and than drive away in vans decorated with clowns and balloons.

Years ago when the movie was initially released (circa 1988) Keel and I went to 42nd Street on Time Square to catch the Chiodo Brother's flick *Killer*

Klowns From Outer Space. In this hysterical horror comedy aliens land in the woods near Santa Cruz for the purpose of taking over the world. Their spaceship looks like a circus Big Top and their ray guns shoot cotton candy that can entangle an unsuspecting earthling.

Now I don't know if Coulrophobia can be inherited. DK Nihoa has never said outright that he is afraid of clowns but he'd have every right to be because of an experience his mother underwent about a quarter of a century ago. I know Nihoa because we both belong to an on line group that gathers material on the bizarre world of inner and hollow earth beings called the Dero. A writer named Richard Sharpe Shaver described them in numerous pulp magazine articles published starting in the mid 1940s, mostly in *Amazing Stories*. Copious books such as the *Hidden World* series keeps the subject alive and those who have information to share on ancient worlds or cavern dwellers in general are welcome to sign up at ShaverMystery@Yahoogroups.com and have a chat with myself and DK as well as the group's moderator Richard Toronto, editor of the Shavertron which can also be found on line.

Anyway, to get to the crux of the matter. this is the story that his mother told him:

"My parents were driving back to Nevada from Los Angeles. My mom was driving the Cadillac, while dad was napping in the passenger side and my nephew who was still a child was in the back seat sleeping.

"Somewhere in the desert possible just north of Lancaster, my mom was driving late at night heading north. There were no other cars on the road. This was back when the highway was just an old two lane black-top road. Suddenly she saw something up ahead in her lane so she swerved into the other lane (still no other cars around) and as she started to pass the object she saw what looked like a 12 foot tall clown walking down the middle of the northbound lane. It stopped and turned around to watch her as she passed it. She said the hair on her neck stood up and she got goose bumps!"

DK insists his mom still talks about the episode. "The family all believe her as mom doesn't make up stuff like this, she's full-blood Western Shoshone and originally Death Valley was where her grandfather lived." As an added note, DK reveals that the incident transpired near the military base Bill Hamilton says underwent a series of sightings (detailed above) and that he feels it might be tied in with a military experiment of some sort.

Hey beg your pardon, but we've never known the U.S. military to clown around like this before! Yuck. Yuck.

Leaping Lizards and A Teleporting Leprechaun
by Paul Dale Roberts

On July 22, 2009, I received a call from Danielle and Christina Day who are sisters recently traveling through the Mojave Desert. One of their hobbies is to collect rocks from the desert. The sisters told me that while sitting under a California fan palm, that they witnessed what they thought was a leprechaun. The leprechaun they said, was actually wearing a greenish type of clothing. If the outfit the leprechaun was wearing were on a regular human being, it would look like the clothes of a homeless person – ragged and somewhat shredded.

What was very peculiar about this leprechaun is that it looked like it was looking for something on the ground and instead of moving from one area to another area, it was basically teleporting anywhere from 3 to 5 feet. It would go from one area, vanish and reappear a distance from its former position. It continued looking at the ground as if it were trying to find something.

Daniel and Christina said they were scared by this experience and hid behind the rock and the palm. I asked the sisters to describe the leprechaun to the best of their ability. They said the leprechaun had black small eyes, a button nose, wrinkled skin and a droopy mouth. The height of the leprechaun was 2 feet, shoes were black and pointed, hands had 5 digits, but seemed to be bloated. Both sisters could not see the leprechaun's teeth. The leprechaun wore a black top hat with a metallic star that seemed to be attached to the side of the head wear.

As the sisters continued to watch the leprechaun, he brought out a small hand held device and it flashed a reddish beam to the ground and the soil became disturbed. The disturbed soil produced a mini whirling sand vortex. After watching the leprechaun for a period of about an hour and a half, it simply vanished into thin air.

From what Danielle and Christina have told me, it appears that the leprechaun they witnessed is an inter-dimensional type of being. It appears it can go into our reality and back into its own reality. I have sometimes wondered if elves, fairies, leprechauns, trolls, pixies are former extraterrestrials that have been stranded here on earth. If they were left behind here, they probably built secret colonies and of course avoid mankind at all costs. Since these little people have the ability to teleport, avoiding humankind would not seem to be an issue. Just a thought.

www.hpiparanormal.net

* * * * * *

And so we have come to the end of the dusty road. Our journey across the Mojave and into the heart of Death Valley is over – at least for the time being. But don't let us stop you from venturing into one of the most beautiful and exotic areas of the United States. Sure you have to be careful of aliens looking to take you for a ride, or a ghostly stagecoach that might accidentally run over your boots. But the upside is that a leprechaun may possible lead you to an abandoned gold mine in the desert and your worries will be over. Regardless, we can almost guarantee you will experience a rainbow in your life somewhere along the way.

The faithful look to the sky for an apparition of the Virgin Mary which supposedly shows up on the 13th of each month in California City.

www.ingramcontent.com/pod-product-compliance
Lightning Source LLC
Chambersburg PA
CBHW081918170426
43200CB00014B/2761